MARTIN VAN BUREN
1782-1862

Chronology-Documents-Bibliographical Aids

Edited by
IRVING J. SLOAN

Series Editor
HOWARD F. BREMER

Oceana Publications, Inc.
Dobbs Ferry, New York
1969

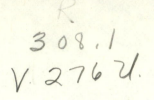

Library of Congress Catalog Card Number 69-15391
Oceana Book No. 303-7

Printed in the United States of America

CONTENTS

EDITOR'S FOREWORD

Every attempt has been made to cite the most accurate dates in this Chronology. Diaries, documents, and similar evidence have been used to determine the exact date. If, however, later scholarship has found such dates to be obviously erroneous, the more plausible date has been used.

This is a research tool compiled primarily for the student. While it does make some judgments on the significance of the events, it is hoped that they are reasoned judgments based on a long acquaintance with American History.

Obviously, the very selection of events by any writer is itself a judgment.

The essence of these books is in their making available some pertinent facts, providing some key documents, and adding a selective, critical bibliography which should direct the student to investigate for himself additional and/or contradictory material. Every effort has been made to cite the best of recent scholarship and, except for classics, to omit old, out of the print works.

Documents in this volume are taken from James D. Richardson, ed., **Messages and Papers of the Presidents**, Vol. III (Washington, D.C., 1897). The complete Special Session Message of September, 1837 is included because of its importance and since it is not as readily accessible as State of the Union messages, recently reprinted in the volumes edited by Fred L. Israel.

CHRONOLOGY

EARLY LIFE

1782

December 5   Born in Kinderhook, near Albany, New York, the third of five children of Abraham and Maria Goes Hoes Van Alen Van Buren.

1796

Graduated from the local village schools at the age of fourteen.
Became a law clerk in the law office of Francis Sylvester, a Federalist.

1800

Sent as delegate to Republican Congressional Caucus in Troy, New York, as a result of his work on behalf of Thomas Jefferson's presidential campaign.

1801

Entered as clerk in the New York City law office of William P. Van Ness. Van Ness was to be a second for Aaron Burr in his duel with Alexander Hamilton, and later a political opponent of Van Buren.

1803

Fall   Admitted to the bar and returned to Kinderhook where he associated himself in practice with his half-brother, James I. Van Alen.

1806

February 20   Breach had developed between followers of Governor Lewis (Lewisites or Quids) and DeWitt Clinton, so Clintonians united with followers of Aaron Burr, or Burrites. Van Buren aligned himself with this new coalition.

February 24   Some disgruntled Burrites and Livingston followers met at a tavern owned by a Tammany member named Abraham Martling. The group became synonymous with the Tammany Society.

1807

February 21   Married Hannah Hoes, childhood sweetheart, in Catskill, New York.

April   Supported Daniel D. Tompkins, nominated by the Tammany-Clintonian faction, for governor against Morgan Lewis.

November 27   First son, Abraham, born in Kinderhook.

1808

February 20   Appointed to his first public office, Surrogate of Columbia County, shortly after Governor Tompkins took office. Displaced his half-brother and partner, James I. Van Alen, who belonged to the defeated faction.

December   Moved his family to Hudson, New York.

1810

February 18   Son, John, born.

1811

January   Participated in a convention in Albany in which Republicans opposed the proposed recharter of the Bank of the United States.

February 20   Vice-President George Clinton cast deciding vote in the United States Senate against the bank bill and Van Buren praised his "Spartan firmness."

November 25   Challenged to a duel by a young lawyer, John Sudam, who backed out after sobering up. Van Buren turned the affair into a triumph over his political opponents.

1812

April   Elected to the New York State Senate over Edward P. Livingston. Van Buren was supported by DeWitt Clinton, later a political enemy, and ran on a platform supporting the war and lauding the defeat of the rechartering of the Bank of the United States.

June 18   Congress declared war against England.

November   At the New York Republican caucus acted as floor leader to secure New York's vote for DeWitt Clinton over James Madison for President.

November 3   Took office in the Senate of New York, serving until 1820.

December 20   Third son, Martin, born.

1813

February   Dissolved political connections with DeWitt Clinton, who was denied the renomination for the office of lieutenant governor by his party.

March 19   Federalist-dominated Council of Appointment removed him from office of Surrogate of Columbia County, making him a victim of the "spoils system" in New York State. The New York "spoils system" was used by both Federalists and Republicans from 1794 on, and the Council of Appointment was largely responsible.

1814

January   Responded to the Governor's Annual Message, defending the War of 1812 against the address to the Governor made by the Federalist Assembly.

September   Introduced "Classification Bill," a draft proposal to conscript New Yorkers according to a class quota, and secured its passage. The war ended before its effectiveness could be tested.

December 24   Treaty of Peace signed with Great Britain at Ghent, ending the War of 1812.

1815

February 17   Appointed Attorney-General of New York State as result of Federalist losses and Republican gains in state elections. Continued to serve as Senator in state Senate.

December   DeWitt Clinton proposed the building of the Erie Canal and restored his popularity.

1816

March 4   Van Buren appointed Regent of the University of the State of New York.

April   Re-elected to New York State Senate. Moved to Albany, forming partnership with Benjamin F. Butler. Van Buren, Butler, William Learned Marcy, Samuel A. Talcott and Edwin Croswell were leaders of a group called the Albany Regency. They controlled the Bucktails, as Tammany supporters were called, getting their name from the tail of a buck worn in their hats at meetings. Croswell was editor of the Regency newspaper, the Albany *Argus*.

November	Governor Tompkins elected Vice-President under James Monroe; governor's office to be vacant in 1817 and leadership of New York Republicans fell to Van Buren.

1817

January 16	Fourth son, Smith Thompson, born.
February 16	Mother died.
April 8	Father died.
April	Van Buren, the "Bucktails," and the Albany Regency unable to prevent DeWitt Clinton winning the governorship by a landslide. Clinton received increasing support from the Federalists, who had little strength as a party.
May	Van Buren voted in favor of construction of Erie Canal in spite of the fact that the measure was promoted by Clinton. Introduced in New York Senate the first bill calling for repeal of imprisonment for debt laws.

1819

February 5	Wife died in Albany at 35. Buried in Kinderhook.
March	Clinton removed him from office as Attorney General of New York. But Van Buren and the Regency still controlled the Assembly, the patronage dealing Council of Appointment, and the Canal Commission.

1820

March	Successfully defended ex-Governor and now Vice-President Daniel D. Tompkins against charges of mishandling public funds while serving as Governor in New York.
April	Promoted the re-election of Rufus King, Federalist, to the United States Senate.
July	Returned to private practice of law in Albany, holding no political office.
November	Chosen presidential elector in New York and voted for James Monroe who was elected President.

1821

February 6	Elected to the United States Senate with the assistance of the Bucktails against the incumbent Senator Nathan Sanford who was supported by the Clintonians and Federalists.

August 28   Bucktails, over Clintonian-Federalist opposition, forced holding of a constitutional convention to amend New York's archaic constitution. Van Buren controlled a solid majority of the delegates and pushed through a liberalization of the suffrage as well as the abolition of the Council of Appointment.

December 21   Took his seat in the United States Senate.

1822

January 7   Lost a bitter fight with Postmaster General Return Jonathan Meigs over an attempt to block the appointment of a former Federalist, General Solomon Van Rensselaer as postmaster of Albany. President Monroe finally backed Meigs.

February 12   Delivered maiden speech in the Senate. While charging fraud on a minor land grant, because of tension was unable to complete the speech.

May 4   Cumberland Road Bill vetoed by President Monroe. Van Buren had voted for the bill, providing funds to repair the road, but was to regret his vote soon after. Internal improvements, part of Henry Clay's "American System," was a Federalist doctrine, he argued.

1823

January   Became Chairman of the Senate Judiciary Committee.

March 30   Decided to accept appointment to the Supreme Court if offered to him. Actually, Monroe had no intention of appointing Van Buren, and appointed Smith Thompson, Secretary of the Navy, who took office in September.

Spring-Summer   Made many trips to Virginia, preparing a New York-Virginia alliance to elect William H. Crawford, the Secretary of the Treasury, as President in 1824.

September   Crawford stricken with paralysis, but Van Buren continued to work for his nomination.

1824

January   Proposed Constitutional amendment removing from House of Representatives the election of President in event candidate did not receive majority, but calling for new election by the electors. Also proposed Constitutional amendment to give Congress power to make internal improvements, but only with consent of states within which improvements were to be made and only under such states' supervision of funds. Congress killed both amendments.

February 14   Republican caucus nominated a ticket of Crawford and Albert Gallatin, but only 66 of 256 Republicans attended. To Van Buren's dismay, "King Caucus" was dead.

February 17   Informed the Regency that Calhoun was about to retire from the presidential race in favor of Jackson. Believed Clay would retire and support Crawford.

April   Regency stupidly removed Clinton from his office as canal commissioner. Public opinion was outraged and returned Clinton to the governorship in November. Van Buren later referred to this as "killing a man too dead."

May   Visited Thomas Jefferson at Monticello, spending several days discussing governmental principles and politics.

November 2   Election day, with Clinton winning and Van Buren's Bucktails losing control of the New York Assembly.

November 16   Van Buren outmaneuvered by Thurlow Weed and anti-Regency factions so that New York's electoral vote was split, with Crawford last.

December 1   Electoral vote in nation gave Jackson 99, Adams 84, Crawford 41, Clay 37. The election was thus up to the House of Representatives to choose from the top three candidates. Calhoun was decisively elected Vice-President, with Georgia casting its 9 votes for Van Buren.

1825

February 9   Adams elected President by House of Representatives with Van Buren unable to deliver key New York vote to prevent his victory.

February 11   Voted against topographical surveys in anticipation of public works by the federal government.

February 23   Voted against appropriation to extend Cumberland Road; reversing his original position of supporting internal improvements, he hereafter consistently opposed federal activity in this area.

March Voted for Henry Clay's confirmation as Secretary of State, although most members of his party, including Andrew Jackson of Tennessee, voted to reject Clay on ground of his alleged "sale" of the presidency to Adams.

November 2 Erie Canal opened. Van Buren did not participate in ceremonies.

1826

February 15 Introduced first of series of proposals to defeat President Adams' Panama Mission, Van Buren's first move against the Administration.

April 7 As Chairman of the Judiciary Committee he brought House bill to Senate floor to revise federal judiciary system which included the addition of three Justices to the Supreme Court. Bill was defeated.

May Voted against construction of the Dismal Swamp Canal. The bill passed.

July 4 Thomas Jefferson and John Adams died.

November Through his political strategems, Van Buren gained control of New York state's electoral votes for the next presidential election.

1827

January 9 Albany *Argus* Regency newspaper, reported the planning of first national political convention in 1828 for purpose of nominating president.

May 12 Returned to Washington after a two months tour of the South, accompanied by Churchill C. Cambreling. He was busy making alliances to turn the Republican party into a truly national party, to be built around Andrew Jackson in a North-South alliance.

July 5-31 Received letters from Thomas Cooper, president of South Carolina College, opposing a protective tariff, and trying to persuade Van Buren that opposing a tariff now might hurt him at the moment but would aid in the long run.

August 3 Convention at Harrisburg, Pennsylvania drew up petition to Congress for tariff increase. Van Buren, not attending, was equivocal because of South's opposition.

September	William Morgan affair led to Anti-Mason movement in Western New York. Van Buren, after touring the area, was convinced it had little national significance.
September 26	Committed the Bucktails and the Regency to Jackson, completing the North-South alliance. This could be marked as the date for the formation of the Democratic Party, although it was not called this for some time.
November	Re-elected Senator by large majorities in both houses of New York legislature.
December	With anti-administration people in control of Congress, Van Buren was the acknowledged majority leader.

1828

January 31	A tariff bill, with high duties on raw materials, especially hemp and wool, introduced in the House by Silas Wright. The idea was Van Buren's, to gather support for Jackson from the West and Middle states. The old thesis that he made it so high that New England would vote it down is denied by historians like Robert V. Remini.
February 11	The sudden death of Governor DeWitt Clinton removed Van Buren's chief rival for political control of New York. Most Clintonians joined the Adams faction.
May 19	"Tariff of Abominations" signed into law. The changing nature of the Northeast with its emphasis on manufacturing, exemplified by Daniel Webster (and Van Buren), was decisive.
July	Agreed to run for Governor of New York in order to strengthen Andrew Jackson's presidential campaign in the state.
November 4	Elected governor of New York, with Enos Throop as lieutenant governor, although their vote was less than that of Smith Johnson, the National Republican candidate, and Francis Granger, the Anti-Mason nominee. Andrew Jackson received twenty of New York's electoral vote to Adams' sixteen.
December 3	Jackson and Calhoun elected President and Vice-President respectively. The new party alignment, with Van Buren a major factor in its creation, was now to be called the

Democratic Party (officially the Democratic-Republican until 1840).

1829

January 1   Inaugurated as governor and resigned as United States Senator.

February 15   Received formal offer from President Jackson to accept appointment as Secretary of State, an agreement made long before.

March 6   Term began as Secretary of State. Stayed at Albany to complete legislative term.

March 12   Resigned as governor, succeeded by Enos Throop.

April 5   Took up duties as Secretary of State. Dominated the cabinet, as well as the "Kitchen Cabinet," Jackson's unofficial advisors.

April 23   Warned Jackson against appointing Samuel Swartwout Collector of the Port of New York. Jackson ignored the excellent advice, and Swartwout embezzled over a million dollars from customhouse funds before fleeing to England in 1838.

May   Called upon Peggy Eaton, wife of Secretary of War John H. Eaton, who was being ostracized by Cabinet members and their wives for alleged scandalous activities. This act in support of the President's expressed wishes cemented relationship between Jackson and Van Buren, as well as adding to the split between Jackson and Calhoun.

December 8   President Jackson, in Annual Message, questioned constitutionality of the Bank of the United States and the Bank war began. Van Buren and his Regency were accused, by Henry Clay and by friends of Calhoun, of conspiring to move the money power from Chestnut Street (Philadelphia) to Wall Street. Nicholas Biddle knew there was little to the conspiracy idea but did fear Van Buren's influence over Jackson.

1830

April 13   Delivered toast at Jefferson Birthday Dinner supporting Jackson's previous toast, declaring for the Union above states' rights as proposed by John Calhoun.

May 7   Negotiated treaty with Turkey giving access to the Black
                     Sea to American shipping.

May 27   Wrote Jackson's veto message on the Maysville Road, in-
                     dicating opposition to internal improvements as well as
                     striking a political blow at Henry Clay, the bill's sponsor.

October 5   Reestablished trade with the West Indies, closed since
                     1825, by securing a treaty with Great Britain.

December   Awarded membership to the Phi Beta Kappa society at
                     Union College.

1831

May 23   Resigned as Secretary of State to give Jackson opportunity
                     to remove entire Cabinet and replace membership with men
                     more loyal to him than to his Vice-President, Calhoun.

June 23   Appointed to serve as Minister to Great Britain.

July 4   Treaty, in which France agreed to pay claims against her
                     arising out of Napoleonic Wars, concluded. Van Buren
                     and the minister to France, William C. Rines, had done
                     much of the spade work.

August 16   Sailed on packet boat, *President*, to Great Britain with
                     son, John, who was an attache at legation in London.
                     Washington Irving was Secretary of the Legation.

1832

January 25   Senate rejected his nomination as Minister to England,
                     with Vice-President Calhoun, casting the deciding vote
                     after a tie.

May 21-23   Democratic National Convention at Baltimore nominated
                     Van Buren for Vice-President to run with Jackson. The
                     "two-thirds rule," requiring candidates to receive two-
                     thirds of the votes of the delegates rather than a simple
                     majority was put into effect to block opposition to Van
                     Buren. It lasted until 1936. Van Buren received 208 of
                     283 votes on the first ballot.

July 5   Arrived in New York from abroad where he had taken a
                     continental trip after concluding his duties in Great Britain.

July 10   Jackson vetoed the bill to recharter the Bank of the United

States. Van Buren's advice to Jackson was to base the reasons on economic, rather than constitutional, grounds.

November 6   Van Buren elected Vice-President with Jackson as President. Thirty electors refused to support Van Buren, but the Jackson landslide carried the day.

1833

March 4   Inaugurated as Vice-President.

March 19   Jackson asked cabinet for opinion on the removal of federal deposits from the Bank of the United States. Van Buren's position was typically equivocal, opposing it at first, but later approving.

December 16   Presided in the Senate for the first time.

1834

April   Whig party formed, a coalition of Jackson's (and Van Buren's) opponents: National Republicans (Adams), States-rights Democrats (Calhoun, John Tyler of Virginia), American System supporters (Clay, Webster), Anti-Masons (William Wirt of Maryland, Thaddeus Stevens of Pennsylvania, Thurlow Weed of New York).

April 15   Jackson protested the Senate's censure for removing deposits from the B.U.S. Van Buren persuaded the President to soften the "Protest," fearing it sounded too much like seizure of executive authority and might harm his own presidential chances in 1836. The softened second protest was submitted to the Senate on April 21.

1835

January 30   Assassination attempt on Jackson led to a period of fear. At one point Van Buren kept two guns on the dais as he presided over the Senate.

May 20-22   Van Buren nominated for President at second national convention of the Democratic party held in Baltimore. Richard M. Johnson of Kentucky nominated for Vice-President.

October 29   Locofocos seized control of Tammany in New York City, and Democrats moved toward the left in economic doctrine.

December 16   William Henry Harrison of Ohio nominated for president by Anti-Masonic party convention held in Harrisburg, Penn. Francis Granger of New York nominated for Vice-President. The Whigs held no national convention, but put up regional candidates in the hope of throwing the election to the House: Daniel Webster of Massachusetts, Hugh L. White of Tennessee, and William P. Mangum of North Carolina.

1836

March 2   Texas declared independence from Mexico during siege of the Alamo. Jackson (and Van Buren) rebuffed annexation attempts because of anti-slavery opposition.

June 23   Jackson signed the Distribution Act, providing for giving federal surplus revenue to the states. He said he had approved this inflationary act to help Van Buren win the presidency.

July 11   The Specie Circular issued by Secretary of the Treasury Levi Woodbury. It had been drafted by Senator Thomas Hart Benton and its issuance ordered by Jackson. It required gold and silver payments for public land, and helped to bring on the Panic of 1837.

November   Presidential campaign ended after much mudslinging and abuse directed against Van Buren, including the biography issued under Davy Crockett's name but actually ghostwritten by a political opponent.

December 7   Van Buren elected President. Received 762,678 popular votes while combined opposing candidates received 735,-650. He received 170 electoral votes; Harrison, 73; White, 26; Webster, 14; Magnum, 11. Richard M. Johnson failed to obtain a majority for Vice-President and for the first and only time the Senate decided the issue for him by a vote of 33 to 16 on February 8, 1837.

1837

January 28   Retired as Vice-President. William R. King, Senator from Albama, elected president *pro tempore* of the Senate.

February   "Flour riots" in New York City, protesting high food prices. A depression was already in evidence, with tight money and unemployment, but most prices of foodstuffs and fuel remained high for months. Cotton prices fell, however, the next month.

March 3	Jackson recognized the independence of Texas, undoubtedly to protect Van Buren from Northern criticism if left until his administration.

TERM IN OFFICE

March 4	Van Buren inaugurated as 8th President, first born a citizen of the United States and therefore never a British subject; also, first President born in New York. All members of Cabinet except one, Joel R. Poinsett of South Carolina, Secretary of War; carried over from Jackson administration. The others were: John Forsyth of Georgia, Secretary of State; Levi Woodbury of New Hampshire, Secretary of Treasury; Mahlon Dickerson of New Jersey, Secretary of Navy; Amos Kendall of Kentucky, Postmaster General; Benjamin F. Butler of New York, Attorney General.
March 6	Nominated Powhaton Ellis of Mississippi to be Minister to Mexico "to be sent whenever circumstances will permit a renewal of diplomatic intercourse honorably with that power."
March 8	Congress had earlier in the year enlarged the Supreme Court from seven to nine members giving Van Buren the opportunity to appoint two new justices and perhaps to liberalize the Court even more. Jackson had appointed Roger B. Taney Chief Justice in 1835 on the death of John Marshall, and Taney had handed down the *Charles River Bridge v. Warren Bridge* decision on February 14, just before Van Buren took office. Van Buren appointed John Catron of Tennessee and William Smith of Alabama. Smith refused to serve and Van Buren appointed John McKinley of Alabama who began to serve on April 22.
March 15	Warned by Senator Nathaniel P. Tallmadge, leader of the conservative faction of New York Democrats, to discard Jackson's hard money policies or lose the 1838 Congressional elections to the Whigs, Tallmadge and Virginia's William Cabell Rives, were to frequently oppose the administration on its fiscal policies.
April 14	Warned in a letter by Thomas Cooper that South must be left alone on slavery—the alternative would be "separation or war."

May 7   Delegation of fifty New York merchants demand Van Buren rescind the Specie Circular, without getting any satisfaction from the President.

May 10   Economic panic begins with suspension of specie payments by New York banks. Depression of 7 years set in; 618 banks failed during first year.

May 15   Van Buren issued Proclamation calling for special session of Congress to meet September 11 to deal with economic crisis.

August 4   Texas formally applied for annexation to the United States. Van Buren discouraged the application.

August 25   Texas petition for annexation refused by Secretary of State Forsyth.

September 4   Special message to Congress blamed depression on speculation and too easy bank credit. Proposed an independent treasury system and temporary issue of treasury notes.

September 14 Independent Treasury Bill introduced in Senate by Silas Wright of New York, a Van Buren supporter.

September 26 Sent House of Representatives the correspondence with Great Britain it had requested on the Maine boundary dispute.

October 2   Fourth installment of distribution of surplus revenue among states suspended because of bank failures.

October 4   Independent Treasury Bill passed by Senate, 26-20, with Calhoun voting for the administrative bill.

October 12   Congress authorized issue of treasury notes up to $10,-000,000 to ease financial situation.

October 14   Independent Treasury Bill tabled in House, 120-106, and extra session ended. Bill defeated June 25, 1838, 125-11.

October 21   Osceola, Seminole Chief, seized while under flag of truce. Died in prison January, 1838, with Van Buren criticized by press.

December 5   First Annual Message to Congress again urged that an Independent Treasury be established.

December 22	Answered the Senate (and the House on December 26) which had requested information about diplomacy with Great Britain regarding Oregon, saying nothing had changed the joint occupancy treaty of 1827. Interest in Oregon was increasing.
December 27	Calhoun introduced pro-slavery and states rights resolutions in the Senate hoping to force Van Buren to support them. Henry Clay, leader of the Whigs, answered, however, and received a harsh attack from Calhoun.
December 29	United States steamboat, *Caroline*, leased to Canadian insurrectionists, seized by Canadian militia on United States side of Niagara River, and one American killed; known as the "*Caroline* Affair" and remained foreign relations issue throughout Van Buren's administration.

1838

January	Appointed George Bancroft, the historian, collector of the port of Boston. Bancroft was now the leader of the Democrats in Massachusetts.
January 5	Van Buren issued Proclamation in Canadian Civil War, warning United States citizens not to aid Canadian revolt. Ordered General Winfield Scott to take command in Maine where the Aroostock War had broken out between Canadians and Americans.
January 8	Requested Congress for funds to defend northern frontier with Canada.
February 14	John Quincy Adams presented 350 petitions before House against slavery and annexation of Texas.
March 14	Van Buren submitted to Senate a treaty of commerce and navigation between the United States and Greece for ratification.
April 11	Benjamin F. Butler resigned from Cabinet as Attorney General.
April 25	Boundary treaty with Texas signed.
June 12	Iowa Territory carved out of Wisconsin territory.
June 25	James K. Paulding of New York appointed Secretary of Navy to succeed Mahlon Dickerson.

July 5	Felix Grundy of Tennessee appointed Attorney General.
July 7	All railroads in United States designated by Congress as postal routes.
November	Eldest son Abraham, his private secretary, married Angelica Singleton, niece of the minister to Great Britain, as well as the niece of Dolly Madison. She served as the White House hostess for the widower President.
November 21	Issued second neutrality proclamation in Canadian insurrection, warning Americans against intervening.
December 3	Delivered Second Annual Message to Congress.
December 6	Special Message advising Congress of steps to make best use of legacy of James Smithson to the United States.

1839

January 21	Submitted to Senate treaty of commerce and navigation with the Netherlands for ratification.
February 4	Henry Clay, in speech to Senate, opposed tampering with slavery and attacked the abolitionists.
February 27	Truce in Aroostock War arranged by General Scott between governors of Maine and New Brunswick, but violations continued.
March 3	Authorized by Congress to call out fifty thousand volunteers to protect American interests in Maine.
March 5	Vetoed Joint Resolution of Congress dealing with distribution of Madison Papers on technical ground that Resolution was not certified by the clerk of the House in which it originated.
June	*L'Amistad* seized by its cargo of negro slaves and they landed at Connecticut. Van Buren instructed the United States District Court for Connecticut that, if it found for the Spanish owners, the Negroes should be hurried to an armed ship which had been sent to carry them back to Cuba. The case was eventually taken to the Supreme Court which in 1841 declared the men free.
June-August	Made political tour through New York state.

November 13 Liberty (Abolitionist) Party organized at Warsaw, New York. Nominated James G. Birney of New York for President and Thomas Earle of Pennsylvania for Vice-President. Although both candidates declined the nominations, they received over 7,000 votes in 1840.

November Democrats received bare majority in House thereby giving administration control of both branches.

December 2 Congress convened. Van Buren delivered Third Annual Message to Congress.

1840

January 11 Henry D. Gilpin of Pennsylvania appointed Attorney General to succeed Felix C. Grundy.

March 31 Van Buren issued Executive Order limiting to a ten-hour day the work of all laborers on federal projects.

April 14 Vicious attack made on Van Buren by Representative Charles Ogle of Pennsylvania. Accused the President of extravagance and of luxuriating in "sloth and effeminacy."

May 4-5 William Henry Harrison of Ohio nominated at Whig Party convention held in Baltimore. John Tyler of Virginia nominated for Vice-President.

May 5-7 Van Buren renominated for President by the Democratic party convention in Baltimore. Three nominees for Vice-President: Richard M. Johnson of Kentucky; Littleton W. Tazewell of Virginia; James K. Polk of Tennessee.

May 16 Amos Kendall resigned from Cabinet as Postmaster General to run Van Buren's campaign.

May 19 John M. Niles of Connecticut appointed Postmaster General.

July 4 Van Buren signed Independent Treasury Act passed by Congress in June.

Fall Presidential campaign, with Whigs utilizing techniques and slogans to deride Van Buren ("Van, Van is a used up man") and build up Harrison ("Tippicanoe and Tyler too"). Van Buren was portrayed as an aristocrat living in luxury in "the Palace" (the White House) while Harrison was in his log cabin drinking hard cider. This could be said to be the first modern election, with two political parties and two national conventions and each supporting a single leader. Both parties were, however, coalitions and with deep schisms to be covered up by evasion and bally-hoo.

November 12   Alexander McLeod, a Canadian, arrested in New York State for murder in the *Caroline* affair and Great Britain lodged a strong protest.

December 5   Van Buren delivered his Fourth Annual Message to Congress.

December 11   Henry Clay introduced resolution in Senate to repeal Independent Treasury Act; amendment substituting endorsement of Act prevailed.

December 26   Secretary of State Forsyth replied to Britain's protest in the McLeod case by arguing that it was a state rather than federal case. Trouble with Britain averted when McLoed was found not guilty on October 12, 1841 in Utica, New York.

1841

February 10   President-elect Harrison visited the White House after Van Buren had set a precedent of calling on the old hero.

March 3   Appointed Peter Vivian Daniel of Virginia to the Supreme Court to replace Philip B. Barbour of Virginia who had died February 25. All of Van Buren's appointments to the Court were from the South.

OUT OF OFFICE

March 4   Van Buren attended the inauguration ceremonies, rather than leaving town as had the two Adams.

April   Spent in New York City, still a hero with Tammany.

April 4   Death of President Harrison. John Tyler now President.

May 8   Returned to Kinderhook; rebuilt his home during the summer and named it "Lindenwald."

June 22   John Van Buren (called "Prince John" by the Whigs), the second eldest son, married Elizabeth Van der Poel.

August 13	Independent Treasury Act repealed.
August 16	Tyler vetoed a bill to recharter a National Bank. When a second bill was vetoed on September 9, Tyler's entire cabinet except Secretary of State Daniel Webster resigned. The Tyler-Clay split seemed to augur will for Van Buren in 1844.
	Emergence of Barnburners, a radical wing of the New York Democrats. The name was an allusion to the farmer who burned his barn to kill the rats. It supported Van Buren (with "Prince John" as a likely heir apparent) and was opposed to banks, canals, and expansion of slavery. The conservative wing of the party came to be called Hunkers because they were "hunkering" for office.
February-May	Made trip to the South visiting Henry Clay at Ashland and Andrew Jackson at the Hermitage.
March 31	Henry Clay resigned from the Senate to devote himself to building up the Whig Party and to secure its nomination in 1844.
June 18	Youngest son, Smith Thompson, married Ellen King James.
August 9	Webster-Ashburton Treaty signed, denounced by Andrew Jackson, but typically with little opposition from Van Buren.
November	Elections brought Democrats to power in Congress, with majority pro Van Buren.

1843

Spent year at Lindenwald, with son John and family, keeping political contacts.

1844

March 22	Publication of letter from Jackson, written in 1843, in the Richmond *Enquirer* favoring the acquisition of Texas created a problem for Van Buren.
April 27	In a long evasive letter published in the Washington *Globe*, Van Buren failed to support the acquisition of Texas, fearing war with Mexico. This cost him the support of Jackson and the South. Henry Clay also opposed annexation, in fact, it is widely believed that he and Van Buren had agreed to keep the issue of the 1844 campaign.

May 1
Whigs met in Baltimore and nominated Henry Clay for President, with Theodore Frelinghuysen of New Jersey for Vice-President.

May 27
Democrats met at Baltimore, adopted the two-thirds rule, but this time it backfired on Van Buren, after helping him in 1832 and 1836. On the first ballot he secured 146 votes, Lewis Cass of Michigan 83, and the rest of the total 266 scattered.

May 29
With the convention deadlocked between Van Buren and Cass, on the eighth ballot James K. Polk of Tennessee was brought forward as a dark horse and received 44 votes. On the ninth ballot New York swung to him and eventually he was unanimously nominated. The news was flashed to Washington in ten seconds by the new telegraph.

May 30
Silas Wright of New York, a Van Buren supporter, nominated for Vice-President but declined, refusing to support a ticket backing the annexation of Texas. George Mifflin Dallas of Pennsylvania was then nominated.

1845

January-February
Polk offered Silas Wright the Treasury post in the cabinet but Wright declined, (he had been elected governor of New York). Polk eventually appointed no Van Buren men to his cabinet, even giving the position of Secretary of War to William Learned Marcy, a New York Hunker. Van Buren declined Polk's offer as Minister to Great Britain.

1846

August 8
Wilmot Proviso introduced to exclude slavery from all territory acquired in war with Mexico, supported by Van Buren's Barnburners.

1847

August 27
Death of Silas Wright left Van Buren as the undoubted leader of Northern Democrats.

1848

April
Decided to take a strong stand on the extension of slavery and wrote a long statement giving his views. It was adopted by the Barnburners as their platform to carry to the Democratic National Convention.

May 22-26	Barnburners and Hunkers sent separate delegations from New York to the Democratic National Convention at Baltimore. On Van Buren's orders, the Barnburners withdrew from the convention when Lewis Cass of Michigan was nominated for President with William O. Butler of Kentucky as his running mate.
June	Barnburners called a state convention at Utica, New York and called for the nomination of Van Buren for President. He reluctantly agreed to accept a nomination. Son, John, played leading role.
June 7-9	Whig Party Convention at Philadelphia nominated Zachary Taylor of Louisiana for President and Millard Fillmore of New York for Vice-President.
August 9-10	Free Soil Party formed by a heterogeneous group of people including Barnburners, Liberty Party men, "Conscience" Whigs and free land advocates. Van Buren nominated for President, with Charles Francis Adams of Massachusetts for Vice-President. The platform called for "free soil, free speech, free labor, and free men."
November 7	For the first time, by act of Congress in 1845, the entire nation voted on the same day. Van Buren failed to carry a single state, receiving 291,263 votes. However, he received more votes in New York than Cass (120,510 to 114,318) thus giving that state and the election to Taylor who received 1,360,101 popular and 163 electoral votes. Cass received 1,220,554 popular votes and 127 electoral votes.

1852

November	Van Buren abandoned Free Soil movement and supported the Democratic nominee, Franklin Pierce.

1853

February 8	Van Buren declined appointment as umpire of the British-American Commission for the adjustment of claims against the two countries for all losses since 1812.
April	Sailed with his son, Martin, for a European tour, the first ex-President to leave the United States.
November	Received by Pope Pius IX in Rome.

1854

June 21	Began work on Autobiography at Villa Falangola in Sorrento, Italy.

1855

March 19   His son, Martin, died in Paris.

March   Returned to retirement in Kinderhook.

1856

November   Reluctantly supported James Buchanan's election for President.

1860

November 6   Voted for the Union electoral ticket which represented in New York the combined opposition to Lincoln.

1861

April 16   Requested by Franklin Pierce, as the senior of the five living ex-Presidents to call a meeting at Philadelphia to offer some plan to save the Union but refused to issue the call.

1862

July 24   Died in Kinderhook and buried in the local cemetery.

DOCUMENTS

INAUGURAL ADDRESS
March 4, 1837

The whole tenor of his Address was to promote an understanding between the North and South since the issues of states' rights and slavery were gaining momentum during this period. His own position was reflected in his remarks that he regarded his election as an indorsement of his opposition as a Senator to attempts by Congress to abolish slavery in the District of Columbia against the wishes of the slaveholding states. He emphasized, moreover, his commitment to a strict interpretation of the Constitution. Finally, he paid high tribute to his predecessor and intimate friend, Andrew Jackson.

Fellow-Citizens: The practice of all my predecessors imposes on me an obligation I cheerfully fulfill—to accompany the first and solemn act of my public trust with an avowal of the principles that will guide me in performing it and an expression of my feelings on assuming a charge so responsible and vast. In imitating their example I tread in the footsteps of illustrious men, whose superiors it is our happiness to believe are not found on the executive calendar of any country. Among them we recognize the earliest and firmest pillars of the Republic—those by whom our national independence was first declared, him who above all others contributed to establish it on the field of battle, and those whose expanded intellect and patriotism constructed, improved, and perfected the inestimable institutions under which we live. If such men in the position I now occupy felt themselves overwhelmed by a sense of gratitude for this the highest of all marks of their country's confidence, and by a consciousness of their inability adequately to discharge the duties of an office so difficult and exalted, how much more must these considerations affect one who can rely on no such claims for favor or forbearance! Unlike all who have preceded me, the Revolution that gave us existence as one people was achieved at the period of my birth; and whilst I contemplate with grateful reverence that memorable event, I feel that I belong to a later age and that I may not expect my countrymen to weigh my actions with the same kind and partial hand.

So sensibly, fellow-citizens, do these circumstances press themselves upon me that I should not dare to enter upon my path of duty did I not look for the generous aid of those who will be associated with me in the various and coordinate branches of the Government; did I not

23

respose with unwavering reliance on the patriotism, the intelligence, and the kindness of a people who never yet deserted a public servant honestly laboring in their cause; and, above all, did I not permit myself humbly to hope for the sustaining support of an ever-watchful and beneficent Providence.

To the confidence and consolation derived from these sources it would be ungrateful not to add those which spring from our present fortunate condition. Though not altogether exempt from embarrassments that disturb our tranquillity at home and threaten it abroad, yet in all the attributes of a great, happy, and flourishing people we stand without a parallel in the world. Abroad we enjoy the respect and, with scarcely an exception, the friendship of every nation; at home, while our Government quietly but efficiently performs the sole legitimate end of political institutions—in doing the greatest good to the greatest number—we present an aggregate of human prosperity surely not elsewhere to be found.

How imperious, then, is the obligation imposed upon every citizen, in his own sphere of action, whether limited or extended, to exert himself in perpetuating a condition of things so singularly happy! All the lessons of history and experience must be lost upon us if we are content to trust alone to the peculiar advantages we happen to possess. Position and climate and the bounteous resources that nature has scattered with so liberal a hand—even the diffused intelligence and elevated character of our people—will avail us nothing if we fail sacredly to uphold those political institutions that were wisely and deliberately formed with reference to every circumstance that could preserve or might endanger the blessings we enjoy. The thoughtful framers of our Constitution legislated for our country as they found it. Looking upon it with the eyes of statesmen and patriots, they saw all the sources of rapid and wonderful prosperity; but they saw also that various habits, opinions, and institutions peculiar to the various portions of so vast a region were deeply fixed. Distinct sovereignties were in actual existence, whose cordial union was essential to the welfare and happiness of all. Between many of them there was, at least to some extent, a real diversity of interests, liable to be exaggerated through sinister designs; they differed in size, in population, in wealth, and in actual and prospective resources and power; they varied in the character of their industry and staple productions, and (in some) existed domestic institutions which, unwisely disturbed, might endanger the harmony of the whole. Most carefully were all these circumstances weighed, and the foundations of the new Government laid upon principles of reciprocal concession and equitable compromise. The jealousies which the smaller States might entertain of the power of the rest were allayed by a rule of representation confessedly unequal at the time, and designed forever to remain so. A natural fear that the broad scope of general legislation might bear upon and unwisely control particular interests was counteracted by limits strictly drawn around the action of the Federal authority, and to the people and the States was left unimpaired their sovereign power over the innumerable subjects embraced in the internal government of a just republic, excepting such only as necessarily appertain to the concerns of the whole confederacy or its intercourse as a united community with the other nations of the world.

This provident forecast has been verified by time. Half a century, teeming with extraordinary events, and elsewhere producing astonishing results, has passed along, but on our institutions it has left no injurious mark. From a small community we have risen to a people powerful in numbers and in strength; but with our increase has gone hand in hand the progress of just principles. The privileges, civil and religious, of the humblest individual are still sacredly protected at home, and while the valor and fortitude of our people have removed far from us the slightest apprehension of foreign power, they have not yet induced us in a single instance to forget what is right. Our commerce has been extended to the remotest nations; the value and even nature of our productions have been greatly changed; a wide difference has arisen in the relative wealth and resources of every portion of our country; yet the spirit of mutual regard and of faithful adherence to existing compacts has continued to prevail in our councils and never long been absent from our conduct. We have learned by experience a fruitful lesson—that an implicit and undeviating adherence to the principles on which we set out can carry us prosperouly onward through all the conflicts of circumstances and vicissitudes inseparable from the lapse of years.

The success that has thus attended our great experiment is in itself a sufficient cause for gratitude, on account of the happiness it has actually conferred and the example it has unanswerably given. But to me, my fellow-citizens, looking forward to the far-distant future with ardent prayers and confiding hopes, this retrospect presents a ground for still deeper delight. It impresses on my mind a firm belief that the perpetutity of our institutions depends upon ourselves; that if we maintain the principles on which they were established they are destined to confer their benefits on countless generations yet to come, and that America will present to every friend of mankind the cheering proof that a popular government, wisely formed, is wanting in no element of endurance or strength. Fifty years ago its rapid failure was boldly predicted. Latent and uncontrollable causes of dissolution were supposed to exist even by the wise and good, and not only did unfriendly or speculative theorists anticipate for us the fate of past republics, but the fears of many an honest patriot overbalanced his sanguine hopes. Look back on these forebodings, not hastily but reluctantly made, and see how in every instance they have completely failed.

An imperfect experience during the struggles of the Revolution was supposed to warrant the belief that the people would not bear the taxation rwquisite to discharge an immense public debt already incurred and to pay the necessary expenses of the Government. The cost of two wars has been paid, not only without a murmur, but with unequaled alacrity.

No one is now left to doubt that every burden will be cheerfully borne that may be necessary to sustain our civil institutions or guard our honor or welfare. Indeed, all experience has shown that the willingness of the people to contribute to these ends in cases of emergency has uniformly outrun the confidence of their representatives.

In the early stages of the new Government, when all felt the imposing influence as they recognized the unequaled services of the first President, it was a common sentiment that the great weight of his character could alone bind the discordant materials of our Government together and save us from the violence of contending factions. Since his death nearly forty years are gone. Party exasperation has been often carried to its highest point; the virtue and fortitude of the people have sometimes been greatly tried; yet our system, purified and enhanced in value by all it has encountered, still preserves its spirit of free and fearless discussion, blended with unimpaired fraternal feeling.

The capacity of the people for self-government, and their willingness, from a high sense of duty and without those exhibitions of coercive power so generally employed in other countries, to submit to all needful restraints and exactions of municipal law, have also been favorably exemplified in the history of the American States. Occasionally, it is true, the ardor of public sentiment, outrunning the regular progress of the judicial tribunals or seeking to reach cases not denounced as criminal by the existing law, has displayed itself in a manner calculated to give pain to the friends of free government and to encourage the hopes of those who wish for its overthrow. These occurrences, however, have been far less frequent in our country than in any other of equal population on the globe, and with the diffusion of intelligence it may well be hoped that they will constantly diminish in frequency and violence. The generous patriotism and sound common sense of the great mass of our fellow-citizens will assuredly in time produce this result; for as every assumption of illegal power not only wounds the majesty of the law, but furnishes a pretext for abridging the libeeties of the people, the latter have the most direct and permanent interest in preserving the landmarks of social order and maintaining on all occasions the inviolability of those constitutional and legal provisions which they themselves have made.

In a supposed unfitness of our institutions for those hostile emergencies which no country can always avoid their friends found a fruitful source of apprehension, their enemies of hope. While they foresaw less promptness of action than in governments differently formed, they overlooked the far more important consideration that with us war could never be the result of individual or irresponsible will, but must be a measure of redress for injuries sustained, voluntarily resorted to by those who were to bear the necessary sacrifice, who would consequently feel an individual interest in the contest, and whose energy would be commensurate with the difficulties to be encountered. Actual events have proved their error; the last war, far from impairing, gave new confidence to our Government, and amid recent apprehensions of a similar conflict we saw that the energies of our country would not be wanting in ample season to vindicate its rights. We may not possess, as we should not desire to possess, the extended and every-ready military organization of other nations; we may occasionally suffer in the outset for the want of it; but among ourselves all doubt upon this great point has ceased, while a salutary experience will prevent a contrary opinion from inviting aggression from abroad.

Certain danger was foretold from the extension of our territory, the multiplication of States, and the increase of population. Our system was supposed to be adapted only to boundaries comparatively narrow. These have been widened beyond conjecture; the members of our Confederacy are already doubled, and the numbers of our people are incredibly augmented. The alleged causes of danger have long surpassed anticipation, but none of the consequences have followed. The power and influence of the Republic have risen to a height obvious to all mankind; respect for its authority was not more apparent at its ancient than it is at its present limits; new and inexhaustible sources of general prosperity have been opened; the effects of distance have been averted by the inventive genius of our people, developed and fostered by the spirit of our institutions; and the enlarged variety and amount of interests, productions, and pursuits have strengthened the chain of mutual dependence and formed a circle of mutual benefits too apparent ever to be overlooked.

In justly balancing the powers of the Federal and State authorities difficulties nearly insurmountable arose at the outset, and subsequent collisions were deemed inevitable. Amid these it was scarcely believed possible that a scheme of government so complex in construction could remain uninjured. From time to time embarrassments have certainly occurred; but how just is the confidence of future safety imparted by the knowledge that each in succession has been happily removed! Overlooking partial and temporary evils as inseparable from the practical operation of all human institutions, and looking only to the general result, every patriot has reason to be satisfied. While the Federal Government has successfully performed its appropriate functions in relation to foreign affairs and concerns evidently national, that of every State has remarkably improved in protecting and developing local interests and individual welfare; and if the vibrations of authority have occasionally tended too much toward one or the other, it is unquestionably certain that the ultimate operation of the entire system has been to strengthen all the existing institutions and to elevate our whole country in prosperity and renown.

The last, perhaps the greatest, of the prominent sources of discord and disaster supposed to lurk in our political condition was the institution of domestic slavery. Our forefathers were deeply impressed with the delicacy of this subject, and they treated it with a forbearance so evidently wise that in spite of every sinister foreboding it never until the present period disturbed the tranquillity of our common country. Such a result is sufficient evidence of the justice and the patriotism of their course; it is evidence not to be mistaken that an adherence to it can prevent all embarrassment from this as well as from every other anticipated cause of difficulty or danger. Have not recent events made it obvious to the slightest reflection that the least deviation from this spirit of forebearance is injurious to every interest, that of humanity included? Amidst the violence of excited passions this generous and fraternal feeling has been sometimes disregarded; and standing as I now do before my countrymen, in this high place of honor and of trust, I can not refrain from anxiously invoking my fellow-citizens never to be deaf to its dictates. Perceiving before my election the deep interest this subject was beginning to excite, I believed it a solemn duty fully to make known my sentiments in regard to it, and now, when every motive for misrepresentation has passed away, I trust that they will be candidly weighed and understood. At least they will be my standard of conduct in the path before me. I then declared that if the desire of those of my countrymen who were favorable to my election was gratified "I must go into the Presidential chair the inflexible and uncompromising opponent of every attempt on the part of Congress to abolish slavery in the District of Columbia against the wishes of the slaveholding States, and also with a determination equally decided to resist the slightest intereference with it in the States where it exists." I submitted also to my fellow-citizens, with fullness and frankness, the reasons which led me to this determination. The result authorizes me to believe that they have been approved and are confided in by a majority of the people of the United States, including those whom they most immediately affect. It now only remains to add that no bill conflicting with these views can ever receive my constitutional sanction. These opinions have been adopted in the firm belief that they are in accordance with the spirit that actuated the venerated fathers of the Republic, and that succeeding experience has proved them to be humane, patriotic, expedient, honorable, and just. If the agitation of this subject was intended to reach the stability of our institutions, enough has occurred to show that it has signally failed, and that in this as in every other instance the apprehensions of the timid and the hopes of the wicked for the destruction of our Government are again destined to be disappointed. Here and there, indeed, scenes of dangerous excitement have occurred, terrifying instances of local violence have been witnessed, and a reckless disregard of the consequences of their conduct has exposed individuals to popular indignation; but neither masses of the people nor sections of the country have been swerved from their devotion to the bond of union and the principles it has made sacred. It will be ever thus. Such attempts at dangerous agitation may periodically return, but with each the object will be better understood. That predominating affection for our political system which prevails throughout our territorial limits, that calm and enlightened judgment which ultimately governs our people as one vast body, will always be at hand to resist and control every effort, foreign or domeetic, which aims or would lead to over-throw our institutions.

What can be more gratifying than such a retrospect as this? We look back on obstacles avoided and dangers overcome, on expectations more than realized and prosperity perfectly secured. To the hopes of the hostile, the fears of the timid, and the doubts of the anxious actual experience has given the conclusive reply. We have seen time gradually dispel every unfavorable foreboding and our Constitution surmount every adverse circumstance dreaded at the outset as beyond control. Present excitement will at all times magnify present dangers, but true philosophy must teach us that none more threatening than the past can remain to be overcome; and we ought (for we have just reason) to entertain an abiding confidence in the stability of our institutions and an entire conviction that if administered in the true form, character, and spirit in which they were established they are abundantly adequate to preserve to us and our children the rich blessings already derived from hem, to make our beloved land for a thousand generations that chosen spot where happiness springs from a perfect equality of political rights.

For myself, therefore, I desire to declare that the principle that will govern me in the high duty to which my country calls me is a strict adherence to the letter and spirit of the Constitution as it was designed by those who framed it. Looking back to it as a sacred instrument care-fully and not easily framed; remembering that it was throughout a work of concession and compromise; viewing it as limited to ntional objects; regarding it as leaving to the people and the States all power not ex-plicitly parted with, I shall endeavor to preserve, protect, and defend it by anxiously referring to its provision for direction in every action. To matters of domestic concernment which it has intrusted to the Federal Government and to such as relate to our intercourse with foreign nations I shall zealously devote myself; beyond those limits I shall never pass.

To enter on this occasion into a further or more minute exposition of my views on the various questions of domestic policy would be as obtru-sive as it is probably unexpected. Before the suffrages of my countrymen were conferred upon me I submitted to them, with great precision, my opinions on all the most prominent of these subjects. Those opinions I shall endeavor to carry out with my utmost ability.

Our course of foreign policy has been so uniform and intelligible as to constitute a rule of Executive conduct which leaves little to my discre-tion, unless, indeed, I were willing to run counter to the lights of ex-perience and the known opinions of my constituents. We sedulously culti-vate the friendship of all nations as the condition most compatible with our welfare and the principles of our Government. We decline alliances as adverse to our peace. We desire commercial relations on equal terms, being ever willing to give a fair equivalent for advantages received. We endeavor to conduct our intercourse with openness and sincerity, prompt-ly avowing our objects and seeking to establish that mutual frankness which is as beneficial in the dealings of nations as of men. We have no disposition and we disclaim all right to meddle in disputes, whether internal or foreign, that may molest other countries, regarding them in their actual state as social communities, and preserving a strict neutrality in all their controversies. Well knowing the tried valor of our people and our exhaustless resources, we neither anticipate nor fear any designed aggression; and in the consciousness of our own just conduct we feel a security that we shall never be called upon to exert our determination never to permit an invasion of our rights without punishment or redress.

In approaching, then, in the presence of my assembled countrymen, to make the solemn promise that yet remains, and to pledge myself that I will faithfully execute the office I am about to fill, I bring with me a settled purpose to maintain the institutions of my country, which I trust will atone for the errors I commit.

In receiving from the people the sacred trust twice confided to my illustrious predecessor, and which he has discharged so faithfully and so well, I know that I can not expect to perform the arduous task with equal ability and success. But united as I have been in his counsels, a daily witness of his exclusive and unsurpassed devotion to his country's welfare, agreeing with him in sentiments which his countrymen have warmly supported, and permitted to partake largely of his confidence, I may hope that somewhat of the same cheering approbation will be found to attend upon my path. For him I but express with my own the wishes of all, that he may yet long live to enjoy the brilliant evening of his well-spent life; and for myself, conscious of but one desire, faithfully to serve my country, I throw myself without fear on its justice and its kindness. Beyond that I only look to the gracious protection of the Divine Being whose strengthening support I humbly solicit, and whom I fervently pray to look down upon us all. May it be among the dispensations of His providence to bless our beloved country with honors and with length of days. May her ways be ways of pleasantness and all her paths be peace!

March 4, 1837.

SPECIAL SESSION MESSAGE ON
NATIONAL ECONOMIC DISTRESS
September 4, 1837

The nation was amid an economic "panic" resulting from some of the Jackson Administration's financial policies as well as some of the manipulations of private bankers. A suspension of a number of New York banks led to bank failures throughout the country during the spring of 1837. Van Buren was under great pressure to call for a special session of Congress to propose a remedy for the crisis. He issued the Proclamation for such a special session on May 15, for convening Congress in September. In the meantime he ordered the Secretary of Treasury to discontinue depositing the government's money in banks that had refused to pay in specie. This was the first indication of what his recommendations to the special session would be. His son, Abraham, delivered his message to Congress. It was as much an appeal to the people to support his revolutionary proposal as it was a message to Congress. After surveying the causes of the panic, its effect on other countries, condemning the present banking system, he proposed the establishment of an independent government treasury. The Panic Session, as this first sitting of the Twenty-fifth Congress became known, adjourned sine die October 16 after enacting two of the Administration's recommendations: empowering the Treasury Department to issue $10,000,000 in interest-bearing notes for the government's current obligations and permitting importers to pay custom duties in paper.

Washington, September 4, 1837.

Fellow-Citizens of the Senate and House of Representatives:

The act of the 23d of June, 1836, regulating the deposits of the public money and directing the employment of State, District, and Territorial banks for that purpose, made it the duty of the Secretary of the Treasury to discontinue the use of such of them as should at any time refuse to redeem their notes in specie, and to substitute other banks, provided a sufficient number could be obtained to receive the public deposits upon the terms and conditions therein presribed. The general and almost simultaneous suspension of specie payments by the banks in May last rendered the performance of this duty imperative in respect to those which had been selected under the act, and made it at the same time impracticable to employ the requisite number of others upon the pre-scribed conditions. The specific regulations established by Congress for the deposit and safe-keeping of the public moneys having thus unexpected-ly become inoperative, I felt it to be my duty to afford you an early opportunity for the exercise of your supervisory powers over the subject.

I was also led to apprehend that the suspension of specie payments, increasing the embarrassments before existing in the pecuniary affairs of the country, would so far diminish the public revenue that the accruing receipts into the Treasury would not, with the reserved five millions, be sufficient to defray the unavoidable expenses of the Government until the usual period for the meeting of Congress, whilst the authority to call upon the States for a portion of the sums deposited with them was too restricted to enable the Department to realize a sufficient amount from that source. These apprehensions have been justified by subsequent results, which render it certain that this deficiency will occur if additional means be not provided by Congress.

The difficulties experienced by the mercantile interest in meeting their engagements induced them to apply to me previously to the actual sus-pension of specie payments for indulgence upon their bonds for duties, and all the relief authorized by law was promptly and cheerfully granted. The dependence of the Treasury upon the avails of these bonds to enable it to make the deposits with the States required by law led me in the outset to limit this indulgence to the 1st of September, but it has since been extended to the 1st of October, that the matter might be submitted to your further direction.

Questions were also expected to arise in the recess in respect to the October installment of those deposits requiring the interposition of Con-gress.

A provision of another act, passed about the same time, and intended to secure a faithful compliance with the obligation of the United States to satisfy all demands upon them in specie or its equivalent, prohibited the offer of any bank note not convertible on the spot into gold or silver at the will of the holder; and the ability of the Government, with millions on deposit, to meet its engagements in the manner thus required by law was rendered very doubtful by the event to which I have referred.

Sensible that adequate provisions for these unexpected exigencies could only be made by Congress; convinced that some of them would be indis-pensably necessary to the public service before the regular period of your meeting, and desirous also to enable you to exercise at the earliest moment your full constitutional powers for the relief of the country, I could not with propriety avoid subjecting you to the inconvenience of assembling at as early a day as the state of the popular representation would permit. I am sure that I have done but justice to your feelings in believing that this inconvenience will be cheerfully encountered in the hope of rendering your meeting conducive to the good of the country.

During the earlier stages of the revulsion through which we have just passed much acrimonious discussion arose and great diversity of opinion existed as to its real causes. This was not surprising. The operations of credit are so diversified and the influences which affect them so numerous, and often so subtle, that even impartial and well-informed persons are seldom found to agree in respect to them. To inherent difficulties were also added other tendencies which were by no means favorable to the discovery of truth. It was hardly to be expected that those who disapproved the policy of the Government in relation to the currency would, in the excited state of public feeling produced by the occasion, fail to attribute to that policy any extensive embarrassment in the monetary affairs of the country. The matter thus became connected with the passions and conflicts of party; opinions were more or less affected by political considerations, and differences were prolonged which might otherwise have been determined by an appeal to facts, by the exercise of reason, or by mutual concession. It is, however, a cheering reflection that circumstances of this nature can not prevent a community so intelligent as ours from ultimately arriving at correct conclusions. Encouraged by the firm belief of this truth, I proceed to state my views, so far as may be necessary to a clear understanding of the remedies I feel it my duty to propose and of the reasons by which I have been led to recommend them.

The history of trade in the United States for the last three or four years affords the most convincing evidence that our present condition is chiefly to be attributed to overaction in all the departments of business—an overaction deriving, perhaps, its first impulses from antecedent causes, but stimulated to its destructive consequences by excessive issues of bank paper and by other facilities for the acquisition and enlargement of credit. At the commencement of the year 1834 the banking capital of the United States, including that of the national bank, then existing, amounted to about $200,000,000, the bank notes then in circulation to about ninety-five millions, and the loans and discounts of the banks to three hundred and twenty-four millions. Between that time and the 1st of January, 1836, being the latest period to which accurate accounts have been received, our banking capital was increased to more than two hundred and fifty-one millions, our paper circulation to more than one hundred and forty millions, and the loans and discounts to more than four hundred and fifty-seven millions. To this vast increase are to be added the many millions of credit acquired by means of foreign loans, contracted by the States and State institutions, and, above all, by the lavish accommodations extended by foreign dealers to our merchants.

The consequences of this redundancy of credit and of the spirit of reckless speculation engendered by it were a foreign debt contracted by our citizens estimated in March last at more than $30,000,000; the extension to traders in the interior of our country of credits for supplies greatly beyond the wants of the people; the investment of $39,500,000 in unproductive public lands in the years 1835 and 1836, whilst in the preceding year the sales amounted to only four and a half millions; the creation of debts, to an almost countless amount, for real estate, in existing or anticipated cities and villages, equally unproductive, and at prices now seen to have been greatly disproportionate to their real value; the expenditure of immense sums in improvements which in many cases have been found to be ruinously improvident; the diversion to other pursuits of much of the labor that should have been applied to agriculture, thereby contributing to the expenditure of large sums in the importation of grain from Europe—an expenditure which, amounting in 1834 to about $250,000, was in the first two quarters of the present year increased to more than $2,000,000; and finally, without enumerating other injuriou results, the rapid growth among all classes, and especially in our great commercial towns, of luxurious habits founded too often on merely fancied wealth, and detrimental alike to the industry, the resources, and the morals of our people.

It was so impossible that such a state of things could long continue that the prospect of revulsion was present to the minds of considerate men before it actually came. None, however, had correctly anticipated its severity. A concurrence of circumstances inadequate of themselves to produce such widespread and calamitous embarrassments tended so greatly to aggravate them that they can not be overlooked in considering their history. Among these may be mentioned, as most prominent, the great loss of capital sustained by our commercial emporium in the fire of December, 1835—a loss the effects of which were underrated at the time because postponed for a season by the great faciliies of credit then existing, the disturbing effects in our commercial cities of the transfers of the public moneys required by the deposit law of June, 1836, and the measures adopted by the foreign creditors of our merchants to reduce their debts and to withdraw from the United States a large portion of our specie.

However unwilling any of our citizens may heretofore have been to assign to these causes the chief instrumentality in producing the present state of things, the developments subsequently made and the actual condition of other commercial countries must, as it seems to me, dispel all remaining doubts upon the subject. It has since appeared that evils similar to those suffered by ourselves have been experienced in Great Britain, on the Continent, and, indeed, throughout the commercial world, and that in other countries as well as in our own they have been uniformly preceded by an undue enlargement of the boundaries of trade, promoted, as with us, by unprecedented expansions of the systems of credit. A reference to the amount of banking capital and the issues of paper credits put in circulation in Great Britain, by banks and in other ways, during the years 1834, 1835, and 1836 will show an augmentation of the paper currency there as much disproportioned to the real wants of trade as in the United States. With this redundancy of the paper currency there arose in that country also a spirit of adventurous speculation embracing the whole range of human enterprise. Aid was profusely given to projected improvements; large investments were made in foreign stocks and loans; credits for goods were granted with unbounded liberality to merchants in foreign countries, and all the means of acquiring and employing credit were put in active operation and extended in their effects to every department of business and to every quarter of the globe. The reaction was proportioned in its violence to the extraordinary character of the events which preceded it. The commercial community of Great Britain were subjected to the greatest difficulties, and their debtors in this country were not only suddenly deprived of accustomed and expected credits, but called upon for payments which in the actual posture of things here could only be made through a general pressure and at the most ruinous sacrifices.

In view of these facts it would seem impossible for sincere inquirers after truth to resist the conviction that the causes of the revulsion in both countries have been substantially the same. Two nations, the most commercial in the world, enjoying but recently the highest degree of apparent prosperity and maintaining with each other the closest relations, are suddenly, in a time of profound peace and without any great national disaster, arrested in their career and plunged into a state of embarrassment and distress. In both countries we have witnessed the same redundancy of paper money and other facilities of credit; the same spirit of speculation; the same partial successes; the same difficulties and reverses, and at length nearly the same overwhelming catstrophe. The most material difference between the results in the two countries has only been that with us there has also occurred an extensive derangement in the fiscal affairs of the Federal and State Governments, occasioned by the suspension of specie payments by the banks.

The history of these causes and effects in Great Britain and the United States is substantially the history of the revulsion in all other commercial countries.

The present and visible effects of these circumstances on the operations of the Government and on the industry of the people point out the objects which call for your immediate attention.

They are, to regulate by law the safe-keeping, transfer, and disbursement of the public moneys; to designate the funds to be received and paid by the Government; to enable the Treasury to meet promptly every demand upon it; to prescribe the terms of indulgence and the mode of settlement to be adopted, as well as collecting from individuals the revenue that has accrued as in withdrawing it from former depositories; and to devise and adopt such further measures, within the constitutional competency of Congress, as will be best calculated to revive the enterprise and to promote the prosperity of the country.

For the deposit, transfer, and disbursement of the revenue national and State banks have always, with temporary and limited exceptions, been heretofore employed; but although advocates of each system are still to be found, it is apparent that the events of the last few months have greatly augmented the desire, long existing among the people of the United States, to separate the fiscal operations of the Government from those of individuals or corporations.

Again to create a national bank as a fiscal agent would be to disregard the popular will, twice solemnly and unequivocally expressed. On no question of domestic policy is there stronger evidence that the sentiments of a large majority are deliberately fixed, and I can not concur with those who think they see in recent events a proof that these sentiments are, or a reason that they should·be, changed.

Events similar in their origin and character have heretofore frequently occurred without producing any such change, and the lessons of experience must be forgotten if we suppose that the present overthrow of credit would have been prevented by the existence of a national bank. Proneness to excessive issues has ever been the vice of the banking system—a vice as prominent in national as in State institutions. This propensity is as subservient to the advancement of private interests in the one as in the other, and those who direct them both, being principally guided by the same views and influenced by the same motives, will be equally ready to stimulate extravagance of enterprise by improvidence of credit. How strikingly is this conclusion sustained by experience! The Bank of the United States, with the vast powers conferred on it by Congress, did not or could not prevent former and similar embarrassments, nor has the still greater strength it has been said to possess under its present charter enabled it in the existing emergency to check other institutions or even to save itself. In Great Britain, where it has been seen the same causes have been attended with the same effects, a national bank possessing powers far greater than are asked for by the warmest advocates of such an institution here has also proved unable to prevent an undue expansion of credit and the evils that flow from it. Nor can I find any tenable ground for the reestablishment of a national bank in the derangement alleged at present to exist in the domestic exchanges of the country or in the facilities it may be capable of affording them. Although advantages of this sort were anticipated when the first Bank of the United States was created, they were regarded as an incidental accommodation, not one which the Federal Government was bound or could be called upon to furnish. This accommodation is now, indeed, after the lapse of not many years, demanded from it as among its first duties, and an omission to aid and regulate commercial exchange is treated as a ground of loud and serious complaint. Such results only serve to exemplify the constant desire among some of our citizens to enlarge the powers of the Government and extend its control to subjects with which it should not interfere. They can never justify the creation of an institution to promote such objects. On the contrary, they justly excite among the community a more diligent inquiry into the character of those operations of trade toward which it is desired to extend such peculiar favors.

The various transactions which bear the name of domestic exchanges differ essentially in their nature, operation, and utility. One class of them consists of bills of exchange drawn for the purpose of transferring actual capital from one part of the country to another, or to anticipate the proceeds of property actually transmitted. Bills of this description are highly useful in the movements of trade and well deserve all the encouragement which can rightfully be given to them. Another class is made up of bills of exchange not drawn to transfer actual capital nor on the credit of property transmitted, but to create fictious capital, partaking at once of the character of notes discounted in bank and of bank notes in circulation, and swelling the mass of paper credits to a vast extent in the most objectionable manner. These bills have formed for the last few years a large proportion of what are termed the domestic exchanges of the country, serving as the means of usurious profit and constituting the most unsafe and precarious paper in circulation. This species of traffic, instead of being upheld, ought to be discountenanced by the Government and the people.

In transferring its funds from place to place the Government is on the same footing with the private citizen and may resort to the same legal means. It may do so through the medium of bills drawn by itself or purchased from others; and in these operations it may, in a manner undoubtedly constitutional and legitimate, facilitate and assist exchanges of individuals founded on real transactions of trade. The extent to which they may be done and the best means of effecting it are entitled to the fullest consideration. This has been bestowed by the Secretary of the Treasury, and his views will be submitted to you in his report.

But it was not designed by the Constitution that the Government should assume the management of domestic or foreign exchange. It is indeed authorized to regulate by law the commerce between the States and to provide a general standard of value or medium of exchange in gold and silver, but it is not its province to aid individuals in the transfer of their funds otherwise than through the facilities afforded by the Post Office Department. As justly might it be called on to provide for the transportation of their merchandise. These are operations of trade. They ought to be conducted by those who are interested in them in the same manner that the incidental difficulties of other pursuits are encountered by other classes of citizens. Such aid has not been deemed necessary in other countries. Throughout Europe the domestic as well as the foreign exchanges are carried on by private houses, often, if not generally, without the assistance of banks; yet they extend throughout distinct sovereignties, and far exceed in amount the real exchanges of the United States. There is no reason why our own may not be conducted in the same manner with equal cheapness and safety. Certainly this might be accomplished if it were favored by those most deeply interested; and few can doubt that their own interest, as well as the general welfare of the country, would be promoted by leaving such a subject in the hands of those to whom it properly belongs. A system founded on private interest, enterprise, and competition, without the aid of legislative grants or regulations by law, would rapidly prosper; it would be free from the influence of political agitation and extend the same exemption to trade itself, and it would put an end to those complaints of neglect, partiality, injustice, and oppression which are the unavoidable results of intereference by the Government in the proper concerns of individuals. All former attempts on the part of the Government to carry its legislation in this respect further than was designed by the Constitution have in the end proved injurious, and have served only to convince the great body of the people more and more of the certain dangers of blending private interests with the operations of public business; and there is no reason to suppose that a repetition of them now would be more successful.

It can not be concealed that there exists in our community opinions and feelings on this subject in direct opposition to each other. A large portion of them, combining great intelligence, activity, and influence, are no doubt sincere in their belief that the operations of trade ought to be assisted by such a connection; they disregard a national bank as necessary for this purpose, and they are disinclined to every measure that does not tend sooner or later to the establishment of such an institution. On the other hand, a majority cf the people are believed to be irreconcilably opposed to that measure; they consider such a concentration of power dangerous to their liberties, and many of them regard it as a violation of the Constitution. This collision of opinion has doubtless caused much of the embarrassment to which the commercial transactions of the country have lately been exposed. Banking has become a political topic of the highest interest, and trade has suffered in the conflict of parties. A speedy termination of this state of things, however desirable, is scarcely to be expected. We have seen for half a century that those who advocate a national bank, by whatever motive they may be influenced, constitute a portion of our community too numerous to allow us to hope for an early abandonment of their favorite plan. On the other hand, they must indeed form an erroneous estimate of the intelligence and temper of the American people who suppose that they have continued on slight or insufficient grounds their persevering opposition to such an institution, or that they can be induced by pecuniary pressure or by any other combination of circumstances to surrender principles they have so long and so inflexibly maintained.

My own views of the subject are unchanged. They have been repeatedly and unreservedly announced to my fellow-citizens, who with full knowledge of them conferred upon me the two highest offices of the Government. On the last of these occasions I felt it due to the people to apprise them distinctly that in the event of my election I would not be able to cooperate in the reestablishment of a national bank. To these sentiments

I have now only to add the expression of an increased conviction that the reestablishment of such a bank in any form, whilst it would not accomplish the beneficial purpose promised by its advocates, would impair the rightful supremacy of the popular will, injure the character and diminish the influence of our political system, and bring once more into existence a concentrated moneyed power, hostile to the spirit and threatening the permanency of our republican institutions.

Local banks have been employed for the deposit and distribution of the revenue at all times partially and on three different occasions exclusively: First, anterior to the establishment of the first Bank of the United States; secondly, in the interval between the termination of that institution and the charter of its successor; and thirdly, during the limited period which has now so abruptly closed. The connection thus repeatedly attempted proved unsatisfactory on each successive occasion, notwithstanding the various measures which were adopted to facilitate or insure its success. On the last occasion, in the year 1833, the employment of the State banks was guarded especially, in every way which experience and caution could suggest. Personal security was required for the safe-keeping and prompt payment of the moneys to be received, and full returns of their condition were from time to time to be made by the depositories. In the first stages the measure was eminently successful, notwithstanding the violent opposition of the Bank of the United States and the unceasing efforts made to overthrow it. The selected banks performed with fidelity and without any embarrassment to themselves or to the community their engagements to the Government, and the system promised to be permanently useful; but when it became necessary, under the act of June, 1836, to withdraw from them the public money for the purpose of placing it in additional institutions or of transferring it to the States, they found it in many cases inconvenient to comply with the demands of the Treasury, and numerous and pressing applications were made for indulgence or relief. As the installments under the deposit law became payable their own embarrassments and the necessity under which they lay of curtailing their discounts and calling in their debts increased the general distress and contributed, with other causes, to hasten the revulsion in which at length they, in common with the other banks, were fatally involved.

Under these circumstances it becomes our solemn duty to inquire whether there are not in any connection between the Government and banks of issue evils of great magnitude, inherent in its very nature and against which no precautions can effectually guard.

Unforeseen in the organization of the Government and forced on the Treasury by early necessities, the practice of employing banks was in truth from the beginning more a measure of emergency than of sound policy. When we started into existence as a nation, in addition to the burdens of the new Government we assumed all the large but honorable load of debt which was the price of our liberty; but we hesitated to weigh down the infant industry of the country by resorting to adequate taxation for the necessary revenue. The facilities of banks, in return for the privileges they acquired, were promptly offered, and perhaps too readily received by an embarrassed Treasury. During the long continuance of a national debt and the intervening difficulties of a foreign war the connection was continued from motives of convenience but these causes have long since passed away; we have no emergencies that make banks necessary to aid the wants of the Treasury; we have no load of national debt to provide for, and we have on actual deposit a large surplus. No public interest, therefore, now requires the renewal of a connection that circumstances have dissolved. The complete organization of our Government, the abundance of our resources, the general harmony which prevails between the different States and with foreign powers, all enable us now to select the system most consistent with the Constitution and most conducive to the public welfare. Should we, then, connect the Treasury for a fourth time with the local banks, it can only be under a conviction that past failures have arisen from accidental, not inherent, defects.

A danger difficult, if not impossible, to be avoided in such an arrangement is made strikingly evident in the very event by which it has now been defeated. A sudden act of the banks intrusted with the funds of the people deprives the Treasury, without fault or agency of the Government, of the ability to pay its creditors in the currency they have by law a right to demand. This circumstance no fluctuation of commerce could have produced if the public revenue had been collected in the legal currency and kept in that form by the officers of the Treasury. The citizen whose money was in bank receives it back since the suspension at a sacrifice in its amount, whilst he who kept it in the legal currency of the country and in his own possession pursues without loss the current of his business. The Government, placed in the situation of the former, is involved in embarrassments it could not have suffered had it pursued the course of the latter. These embarrassments are, moreover, augmented by those salutary and just laws which forbid it to use a depreciated currency, and by so doing take from the Government the ability which individuals have of accommodating their transactions to such a catastrophe.

A system which can in a time of profound peace, when here is a large revenue laid by, thus suddenly prevent the application and the use of the money of the people in the manner and for the objects they have directed can not be wise; but who can think without painful reflection that under it the same unforeseen events might have befallen us in the midst of a war and taken from us at the moment when most wanted the use of those very means which were treasured up to promote the national welfare and guard our national rights? To such embarrassments and to such dangers will this Government be always exposed whilst it takes the moneys raised for and necessary to the public service out of the hands of its own officers and converts them into a mere right of action against corporations intrusted with the possession of them. Nor can such results be effectually guarded against in such a system without investing the Executive with a control over the banks themselves, whether State or national, that might with reason be objected to. Ours is probably the only Government in the world that is liable in the management of its fiscal concerns to occurrences like these.

But this imminent risk is not the only danger attendant on the surrender of the public money to the custody and control of local corporations. Though the object is aid to the Treasury, its effect may be to introduce into the operations of the Government influences the most subtle, founded on interests the most selfish.

The use by the banks, for their own benefit, of the money deposited with them has received the saction of the Government from the commencement of this connection. The money received from the people, instead of being kept till it is needed for their use, is, in consequence of this authority, a fund on which discounts are made for the profit of those who happen to be owners of stock in the banks selected as depositories. The supposed and often exaggerated advantages of such a boon will always cause it to be sought for with avidity. I will not stop to consider on whom the patronage incident to it is to be conferred. Whether the selection and control be trusted to Congress or to the Executive, either will be subjected to appeals made in every form which the sagacity of interest can suggest. The banks under such a system are stimulated to make the most of their fortunate acquisition; the deposits are treated as an increase of capital; loans and circulation are rashly augmented, and when the public exigencies require a return it is attended with embarrassments not provided for nor foreseen. Thus banks that thought themselves most fortunate when the public funds were received find themselves most embarrassed when the season of payment suddenly arrives.

Unfortunately, too, the evils of the system are not limited to the banks. It simulated a general rashness of enterprise and aggravates the fluctuations of commerce and the currency. This result was strikingly exhibited during the operations of the late deposit system, and especially in the purchases of public lands. The order which ultimately directed the payment of gold and silver in such purchases greatly checked, but could not altogether prevent, the evil. Specie was indeed more difficult to be procured than the notes which the banks could themselves create at pleasure; but still, being obtained from them as a loan and returned as a deposit, which they were again at liberty to use, it only passed round the circle with diminished speed. This operation could not have been performed had the funds of the Government gone into the Treasury to be regularly disbursed, and not into banks to be loanded out for their own profit while they were permitted to substitute for it a credit in account.

In expressing these sentiments I desire not to undervalue the benefits of a salutary credit to any branch of enterprise. The credit bestowed on probity and industry is the just reward of merit and an honorable incentive to further acquisition. None opposes it who love their country and understand its welfare. But when it is unduly encouraged; when it is made to inflame the public mind with the temptations of sudden and unsubstantial wealth; when it turns industry into paths that lead sooner or later to disappointment and distress, it becomes liable to censure and needs correction. Far from helping probity and industry, the ruin to which it leads falls most severely on the great laboring classes, who are thrown suddenly out of employment, and by the failure of magnificent schemes never intended to enrich them are deprived in a moment of their only resource. Abuses of credit and excesses in speculation will happen despite of the most salutary laws; no government, perhaps, can altogether prevent them, but surely every government can refrain from contributing the stimulus that calls them into life.

Since, therefore, experience has shown that to lend the public money to the local banks is hazardous to the operations of the Government, at least of doubtful benefit to the institutions themselves, and productive of disastrous derangement in the business and currency of the country, is it the part of wisdom again to renew the connection?

It is true that such an agency is in many respects convenient to the Treasury, but it is not indispensable. A limitation of the expenses of the Government to its actual wants, and of the revenue to those expenses, with convenient means for its prompt application to the purposes for which it was raised, are the objects which we should seek to accomplish. The collection, safe-keeping, transfer, and disbursement of the public money can, it is believed, be well managed by officers of the Government. Its collection, and to a great extent its disbursement also, have indeed been hitherto conducted solely by them, neither national nor State banks, when employed, being required to do more than keep it safely while in their custody, and transfer and pay it in such portions and at such times as the Treasury shall direct.

Surely banks are not more able than the Government to secure the money in their possession against accident, violence, or fraud. The assertion that they are so must assume that a vault in a bank is stronger than a vault in the Treasury, and that directors, cashiers, and clerks not selected by the Government nor under its control are more worthy of confidence than officers selected from the people and responsible to the Government—officers bound by official oaths and bonds for a faithful performance of their duties, and constantly subject to the supervision of Congress.

The difficulties of transfer and the aid heretofore rendered by banks have been less than is usually supposed. The actual accounts show that by far the larger portion of payments is made within short or convenient distances from the places of collection; and the whole number of warrants issued at the Treasury in the year 1834—a year the result of which will, it is believed, afford a safe test for the future—fell short of 5,000, or an average of less than 1 daily for each State; in the city of New York they did not average more than 2 a day, and at the city of Washington only 4.

The difficulties heretofore existing are, moreover, daily lessened by an increase in the cheapness and facility of communications, and it may be asserted with confidence that the necessary transfers, as well as the safe-keeping and disbursements of the public moneys, can be with safety and convenience accomplished through the agencies of Treasury officers. This opinion has been in some degree confirmed by actual experience since the discontinuance of the banks as fiscal agents in May last—a period which from the embarrassments in commercial intercourse presented obstacles as great as any that may be hereafter apprehended.

The manner of keeping the public money since that period is fully stated in the report of the Secretary of the Treasury. That officer also suggests the propriety of assigning by law certain additional duties to existing establishments and officers, which, with the modifications and safeguards referred to by him, will, he thinks, enable the Department to continue to perform this branch of the public service without any material addition either to their number or to the present expense. The extent of the business to be transacted has already been stated; and in respect to the amount of money with which the officers employed would be intrusted at any one time, it appears that, assuming a balance of five millions to be at all times kept in the Treasury, and the whole of it left in the hands of the collectors and receivers, the proportion of each would not exceed an average of $30,000; but that, deducting one million for the use of the Mint and assuming the remaining four millions to be in the hands of one-half of the present number of officers—a supposition deemed more likely to correspond with the fact—the sum in the hands of each would still be less than the amount of the bonds now taken from the receivers of public money. Every apprehension, however, on the subject, either in respect to the safety of the money or the faithful discharge of these fiscal transactions, may, it appears to me, be effectually removed by adding to the present means of the Treasury the establishment by law at a few important points of offices for the deposit and disbursement of such portions of the public revenue as can not with obvious safety and convenience be left in the possession of the collecting officers until paid over by them to the public creditors. Neither the amounts retained in their hands nor those deposited in the offices would in an ordinary condition of the revenue by larger in most cases than those often under the control of disbursing officers of the Army and Navy, and might be made entirely safe by requiring such securities and exercising such controlling supervision as Congress may by law prescribe. The principal officers whose appointments would become necessary under this plan, taking the largest number suggested by the Secretary of the

Treasury, would not exceed ten, nor the additional expenses, at the same estimate, $60,000 a year.

There can be no doubt of the obligation of those who are intrusted with the affairs of Government to conduct them with as little cost to the nation as is consistent with the public interest; and it is for Congress, and ultimately for the people, to decide whether the benefits to be derived from keeping our fiscal concerns apart and severing the connection which has hitherto existed between the Government and banks offer sufficient advantages to justify the necessary expenses. If the object to be accomplished is deemed important to the future welfare of the country, I can not allow myself to believe that the addition to the public expenditure of comparatively so small an amount as will be necessary to effect it will be objected to by the people.

It will be seen by the report of the Postmaster-General herewith communicated that the fiscal affairs of that Department have been successfully conducted since May last upon the principle of dealing only in the legal currency of the United States, and that it needs no legislation to maintain its credit and facilitate the management of its concerns, the existing laws being, in the opinion of that officer, ample for those objects.

Difficulties will doubtless be encountered for a season and increased services required from the public functionaries; such are usually incident to the commencement of every system, but they will be greatly lessened in the progress of its operations.

The power and influence supposed to be connected with the custody and disbursement of the public money are topics on which the public mind is naturally, and with great propriety, peculiarly sensitive. Much has been said on them in reference to the proposed separation of the Government from the banking institutions; and surely no one can object to any appeals or animadversions on the subject which are consistent with facts and evince a proper respect for the intelligence of the people. If a Chief Magistrate may be allowed to speak for himself on such a point, I can truly say that to me nothing would be more acceptable than the withdrawal from the Executive, to the greatest practicable extent, of all concern in the custody and disbursement of the public revenue; not that I would shrink from any responsibility cast upon me by the duties of my office, but because it is my firm belief that its capacity for usefulness is in no degree promoted by the possession of any patronage not actually necessary to the performance of those duties. But under our present form of government the intervention of the executive officers in the custody and disbursement of the public money seems to be unavoidable; and before it can be. admitted that the influence and power of the Executive would be increased by dispensing with the agency of banks the nature of that intervention in such an agency must be carefully regarded, and a comparison must be instituted between its extent in the two cases.

The revenue can only be collected by officers appointed by the President with the advice and consent of the Senate. The public moneys in the first instance must therefore in all cases pass through hands selected by the Executive. Other officers appointed in the same way, or, as in some cases, by the President alone, must also be intrusted with them when drawn for the purpose of disbursement. It is thus seen that even when banks are employed the public funds must twice pass through the hands of executive officers. Besides this, the head of the Treasury Department, who also holds office at the pleasure of the President, and some other officers of the same Department, must necessarily be invested with more or less power in the selection, continuance, and supervision of the banks that may be employed. The question is then narrowed to the single point whether in the intermediate stage between the collection and disbursement of the public money the agency of banks is necessary to avoid a dangerous extension of the patronage and influence of the Executive. But is it clear that the connection of the Executive with powerful moneyed institutions, capable of ministering to the interests of men in points where they are most accessible to corruption, is less liable to abuse than his constitutional agency in the appointment and control of the few public officers required by the proposed plan? Will the public money when in their hands be necessarily exposed to any improper interference on the part of the Executive? May it not be hoped that a prudent fear of public jealousy and disapprobation in a matter so peculiarly exposed to them will deter him from any such interference, even if higher motives be found inoperative? May not Congress so regulate by law the duty of those officers and subject it to such supervision and publicity as to prevent the possibility of any serious abuse on the part of the Executive? And is there equal room for such supervision and publicity in a connection with banks, acting under the shield of corporate immunities and conducted by persons irresponsible to the Government and the people? It is believed that a considerate and candid investigation of these questions will result in the conviction that the proposed plan is far less liable to objection on the score of Executive patronage and control than any bank agency that has been or can be devised.

With these views I leave to Congress the measures necessary to regulate in the present emergency the safe-keeping and transfer of the public moneys. In the performance of constitutional duty I have stated to them without reserve the result of my own reflections. The subject is of great importance, and one on which we can scarcely expect to be as united in sentiment as we are in interest. It deserves a full and free discussion, and can not fail to be benefited by a dispassionate comparison of opinions. Well aware myself of the duty of reciprocal concession among the coordinate branches of the Government, I can promise a reasonable spirit of cooperation, so far as it can be indulged in without the surrender of constitutional objections which I believe to be well founded. Any system that may be adopted should be subjected to the fullest legal provision, so as to leave nothing to the Executive but what is necessary to the discharge of the duties imposed on him; and whatever plan may be ultimately established, my own part shall be so discharged as to give to it a fair trial and the best prospect of success.

The character of the funds to be received and disbursed in the transactions of the Government likewise demands your most careful consideration.

There can be no doubt that those who framed and adopted the Constitution, having in immediate view the depreciated paper of the Confederacy—of which $500 in paper were at times only equal to $1 in coin—intended to prevent the recurrence of similar evils, so far at least as related to the transactions of the new Government. They gave to Congress express powers to coin money and to regulate the value thereof and of foreign coin; they refused to give it power to establish corporations—the agents then as now chiefly employed to create a paper currency; they prohibited the States from making anything but gold and silver a legal tender in payment of debts; and the First Congress directed by positive law that the revenue should be received in nothing but gold and silver.

Public exigency at the outset of the Government, without direct legislative authority, led to the use of banks as fiscal aids to the Treasury. In admitted deviation from the law, at the same period and under the same exigency, the Secretary of the Treasury received their notes in payment of duties. The sole ground on which the practice thus commenced was then or has since been justified is the certain immediate, and convenient exchange of such notes for specie. The Government did, indeed; receive the inconvertible notes of State banks during the difficulties of war, and the community submitted without a murmur to the unequal taxation and multiplied evils of which such a course was productive. With the war this indulgence ceased, and the banks were obliged again to redeem their notes in gold and silver. The Treasury, in accordance with previous practice, continued to dispense with the currency required by the act of 1789, and took the notes of banks in full confidence of their being paid in specie on demand; and Congress, to guard against the slightest violation of this principle, have declared by law that if notes are paid in the transactions of the Government it must be under such circumstances as to enable the holder to convert them into specie without depreciation or delay.

Of my own duties under the existing laws, when the banks suspended specie payments, I could not doubt. Directions were immediately given to prevent the reception into the Treasury of anything but gold and silver, or its equivalent, and every practicable arrangement was made to preserve the public faith by similar or equivalent payments to the public creditors. The revenue from lands had been for some time substantially so collected under the order issued by directions of my predecessor. The effects of that order had been so salutary and its forecast in regard to the increasing insecurity of bank paper had become so apparent that even before the catastrophe I had resolved not to interfere with its operation. Congress is now to decide whether the revenue shall continue to be so collected or not.

The receipt into the Treasury of bank notes not redeemed in specie on demand will not, I presume, be sanctioned. It would destroy without the excuse of war or public distress that equality of imposts and identity of commercial regulation which lie at the foundation of our Confederacy, and would offer to each State a direct temptation to increase its foreign trade by depreciating the currency received for duties in its ports. Such a proceeding would also in a great degree frustrate the policy so highly cherished of infusing into our circulation a larger proportion of the precious metals—a policy the wisdom of which none can doubt, though there may be different opinions as to the extent to which it should be carried. Its results have been already too auspicious and its success is too closely interwoven with the future prosperity of the country to permit us for a moment to contemplate its abandonment. We have seen under its influence our specie augmented beyond eighty millions, our coinage increased so as to make that of gold amount, between August, 1834, and December, 1836, to $10,000,000, exceeding the whole coinage at the Mint during the thrity-one previous years.

The prospect of further improvement continued without abatement until the moment of the suspension of specie payments. This policy has now, indeed, been suddenly checked, but is still far from being overthrown. Amidst all conflicting theories, one position is undeniable—the precious metals will invariably disappear when there ceases to be a necessity for their use as a circulating medium. It was in strict accordance with this truth that whilst in the month of May last they were everywhere seen and were current for all ordinary purposes they disappeared from circulation the moment the payment of species was refused by the banks and the community tacitly agreed to dispense with its employment. Their place was supplied by a currency exclusively of paper, and in many cases of the worst description. Already are the bank notes now in circulation greatly depreciated, and they fluctuate in value between one place and another, thus diminishing and making uncertain the worth of property and the price of labor, and failing to subserve, except at a heavy loss, the purposes of business. With each succeeding day the metallic currency decreases; by some it is hoarded in the natural fear that once parted with it can not be replaced, while by others it is diverted from its more legitimate uses for the sake of gain. Should Congress sanction this condition of things by making irredeemable paper money receivable in payment of public dues, a temporary check to a wise and salutary policy will in all probability be converted into its absolute destruction.

It is true that bank notes actually convertible into specie may be received in payment of the revenue without being liable to all these objections, and that such a course may to some extent promote individual convenience —an object always to be considered where it does not conflict with the principles of our Government or the general welfare of the country. If such notes only were received, and always under circumstances allowing their early presentation for payment, and if at short and fixed periods they were converted into specie to be kept by the officers of the Treasury, some of the most serious obstacles to their reception would perhaps be removed. To retain the notes in the Treasury would be to renew under another form the loans of public money to the banks, and the evils consequent thereon.

It is, however, a mistaken impression that any large amount of specie is required for public payments. Of the seventy or eighty millions now estimated to be in the country, ten millions would be abundantly sufficient for that purpose provided an accumulation of a large amount of revenue beyond the necessary wants of the Government be hereafter prevented. If to these considerations be added the facilities which will arise from enabling the Treasury to satisfy the public creditors by its drafts or notes receivable in payment of the public dues, it may be safety assumed that no motive of convenience to the citizen requires the reception of bank paper.

To say that the refusal of paper money by the Government introduces an unjust discrimination between the currency received by it and that used by individuals in their ordinary affairs, is in my judgment, to view it in a very erroneous light. The Constitution prohibits the States from making anything but gold and silver a tender in the payment of debts, and thus secures to every citizen a right to demand payment in the legal currency. To provide by law that the Government will only receive its dues in gold and silver is not to confer on it any peculiar privilege, but merely to place it on an equality with the citizen by reserving to it a right secured to him by the Constitution. It is doubtless for this reason that the principle has been sanctioned by successive laws from the time of the first Congress under the Constitution down to the last. Such precedents, never objected to and proceeding from such sources, afford a decisive answer to the imputation of inequality or injustice.

But in fact the measure is one of restriction, not of favor. To forbid the public agent to receive in payment any other than a certain kind of money is to refuse him a discretion possessed by every citizen. It may be left to those who have the management of their own transactions to make their own terms, but no such discretion should be given to him who acts merely as an agent of the people—who is to collect what the law requires and to pay the appropriations it makes. When bank notes are redeemed on demand, there is then no discrimination in reality, for the individual who receives them may at his option substitute the specie for them; he takes them from convenience or choice. When they are not so redeemed, it will scarcely be contended that their receipt and payment by a public officer should be permitted, though none deny that right to an individual; if it were, the effect would be most injurious to the public, since their officer could make none of those arrangements to meet or guard against the depreciation which an individual is at liberty to do. Nor can inconvenience to the community be alleged as an objection to such a regulation. Its object and motive are their convenience and welfare.

If at a moment of simultaneous and unexpected suspension by the banks it adds something to the many embarrassments of that proceeding, yet these are far overbalanced by its direct tendency to produce a wider circulation of gold and silver, to increase the safety of bank paper, to improve the general currency, and thus to prevent altogether such occurrences and the other and far greater evils that attend them.

It may indeed be questioned whether it is not for the interest of the banks themselves that the Government should not receive their paper. They would be conducted with more caution and on sounder principles. By using specie only in its transactions the Government would create a demand for it, which would to a great extent prevent its exportation, and by keeping it in circulation maintain a broader and safer basis for the paper currency. That the banks would thus be rendered more sound and the community more safe can not admit of a doubt.

The foregoing views, it seems to me, do but fairly carry out the provisions of the Federal Constitution in relation to the currency, as far as relates to the public revenue. At the time that instrument was framed there were but three or four banks in the United States, and had the extension of the banking system and the evils growing out of it been foreseen they would probably have been specially guarded against. The same policy which led to the prohibition of bills of credit by the States would doubtless in that event have also interdicted their issue as a currency in any other form. The Constitution, however, contains no such prohibition; and since the States have exercised for nearly half a century the power to regulate the business of banking, it is not to be expected that it will be abandoned. The whole matter is now under discussion before the proper tribunal—the people of the States. Never before has the public mind been so thoroughly awakened to a proper sense of its importance; never has the subject in all its bearings been submitted to so searching an inquiry. It would be distrusting the intelligence and virtue of the people to doubt the speedy and efficient adoption of such measures of reform as the public good demands. All that can rightfully be done by the Federal Government to promote the accomplishment of that important object will without doubt be performed.

In the meantime it is our duty to provide all the remedies against a depreciated paper currency which the Constitution enables us to afford. The Treasury Department on several former occasions has suggested the propriety and importance of a uniform law concerning bankruptcies of corporations and other bankers. Through the instrumentality of such a law a salutary check may doubtless be imposed on the issues of paper money and an effectual remedy given to the citizen in a way at once equal in all parts of the Union and fully authorized by the Constitution.

The indulgence granted by Executive authority in the payment of bonds for duties has been already mentioned. Seeing that the immediate enforcement of these obligations would subject a large and highly respectable portion of our citizens to great sacrifices, and believing that a temporary postponement could be made without detriment to other interests and with increased certainty of ultimate payment, I did not hestitate to comply with the request that was. made of me. The terms allowed are the full extent as liberal as any that are to be found in the practice of the executive department. It remains for Congress to decide whether a further postponement may not with propriety be allowed; and if so, their legislation upon the subject is respectfully allowed.

The report of the Secretary of the Treasury will exhibit the condition of these debts, the extent and effect of the present indulgence, the probable result of its further extension on the state of the Treasury, and every other fact necessary to a full consideration of the subject. Similar information is communicated in regard to such depositories of the public moneys as are indebted to the Government, in order that Congress may also adopt the proper measures in regard to them.

The receipts and expenditures for the first half of the year and an estimate of those for the residue will be laid before you by the Secretary of the Treasury. In his report of December last it was estimated that the current receipts would fall short of the expenditures by about $3,000,000. It will be seen that the difference will be much greater. This is to be attributed not only to the occurrence of greater pecuniary embarrassments in the business of the country that those which were then predicted, and consequently a greater diminution in the revenue, but also to the fact that the appropriations exceeded by nearly six millions the amount which was asked for in the estimates then submitted. The sum necessary for the service of the year, beyond the probable receipts and the amount which it was intended should be reserved in the Treasury at the commencement of the year, will be about six millions. If the whole of the reserved balance be not at once applied to the current expenditures, but four millions be still kept in the Treasury, as seems most expedient for the uses of the Mint and to meet contingencies, the sum needed will be ten millions.

In making this estimate the receipts are calculated on the supposition of some further extension of the indulgence granted in the payment of bonds for duties; which will affect the amount of the revenue for the present year to the extent of two and a half millions.

It is not proposed to procure the required amount by loans or increased taxation. There are now in the Treasury $9,367,214, directed by the act of the 23d of June, 1836, to be deposited with the States in October next. This sum, if so deposited, will be subject under the law to be recalled if needed to defray existing appropriations; and as it is now evident that the whole, or the principal part, of it will be wanted for that purpose, it appears most proper that the deposit should be withheld. Until the amount can be collected from the banks, Treasury notes may be temporarily issued, to be gradually redeemed as it is received.

I am aware that this course may be productive of inconvenience to many of the States. Relying upon the acts of Congress which held out to them the strong probability, if not the certainty, of receiving this installment, they have in some instances adopted measures with which its retention may seriously interfere. That such a condition of things should have occurred is much to be regretted. It is not the least among the unfortunate results of the disasters of the times; and it is for Congress to devise a fit remedy, if there be one. The money being indispensable to the wants of the Treasury, it is difficult to conceive upon what principle of justice or expediency its application to that object can be avoided. To recall any portion of the sums already deposited with the States would be more inconvenient and less efficient. To burden the country with increased taxation when there is in fact a large surplus revenue would be unjust and unwise; to raise moneys by loans under such circumstances, and thus to commence a new national debt, would scarcely be sanctioned by the American people.

The plan proposed will be adequate to all our fiscal operations during the remainder of the year. Should it be adopted, the Treasury, aided by the ample resources of the country, will be able to discharge punctually every pecuniary obligation. For the future all that is needed will be that caution and forbearance in appropriations which the diminution of the revenue requires and which the complete accomplishment or great forwardness of many expensive national undertakings renders equally consistent with prudence and patriotic liberality.

The preceding suggestions and recommendations are submitted in the belief that their adoption by Congress will enable the executive department to conduct our fiscal concerns with success so far as their management has been committed to it. Whilst the objects and the means proposed to attain them are within its constitutional powers and appropriate duties, they will at the same time, it is hoped, by their necessary operation, afford essential aid in the transaction of individual concerns, and thus yield relief to the people at large in a form adapted to the nature of our Government. Those who look to the action of this Government for specific aid to the citizen to relieve embarrassments arising from losses by revulsions in commerce and credit lose sight of the ends for which it was created and the powers with which it is clothed. It was established to give security to us all in our lawful and honorable pursuits, under the lasting safeguard of republican institutions. It was not intended to confer special favors on individuals or on any classes of them, to create systems of agriculture, manufacturers, or trade, or to engage in them either separately or in connection with individual citizens or organized associations. If its operations were to be directed for the benefit of any one class, equivalent favors must in justice be extended to the rest, and the attempt to bestow such favors with an equal hand, or even to select those who should most deserve them, would never be successful.

All communities are apt to look to government for too much. Even in our own country, where its powers and duties are so strictly limited, we are prone to do so, especially at periods of sudden embarrassment and distress. But this ought not to be. The framers of our excellent Constitution and the people who approved it with calm and sagacious deliberation acted at the time on a sounder principle. They wisely judged that the less government interferes with private pursuits the better for the general prosperity. It is not its legitimate object to make men rich or to repair by direct grants of money or legislation in favor of particular pursuits losses not incurred in the public service. This would be substantially to use the property of some for the benefit of others. But its real duty—that duty the performance of which makes a good government the most precious of human blessings—is to enact and enforce a system of general laws commensurate with, but not exceeding, the objects of its establishment, and to leave every citizen and every interest to reap under its benign protection the rewards of virtue, industry, and prudence.

I can not doubt that on this as on all similar occasions the Federal Government will finds its agency most conducive to the security and happiness of the people when limited in the exercise of its conceded powers. In never assuming, even for a well-meant object, such powers as were not designed to be conferred upon it, we shall in reality do most for the general welfare. To avoid every unnecessary intereference with the pursuits of the citizen will result in more benefit than to adopt measures which could only assist limited interests, and are eagerly, but perhaps naturally, sought for under the pressure of temporary circumstances. If, therefore, I refrain from suggesting to Congress any specific plan for regulating the exchanges of the country, relieving mercantile embarrassments, or interfering with the ordinary operations of foreign or domestic commerce, it is from a conviction that such measures are not within the constitutional province of the General Government, and that their adoption would not promote the real and permanent welfare of those they might be designed to aid.

The difficulties and distresses of the times, though unquestionably great, are limited in their extent, and can not be regarded as affecting the permanent prosperity of the nation. Arising in a great degree from the transactions of foreign and domestic commerce, it is upon them that they have chiefly fallen. The great agricultural interest has in many parts of the country suffered comparatively little, and, as if Providence intended to display the munifence of its goodness at the moment of our greatest need, and in direct contrast to the evils occasioned by the waywardness of man, we have been blessed throughout our extended territory with a season of general health and of uncommon fruitfulness. The proceeds of our great staples will soon furnish the means of liquidating debts at home and abroad, and contribute equally to the revival of commercial activity and the restoration of commercial credit. The banks, established avowedly for its support, deriving their profits from it, and resting under obligations to it which can not be overlooked, will feel at once the necessity and justice of uniting their energies with those of the mercantile interest.

The suspension of specie payments at such a time and under such circumstances as we have lately witnessed could not be other than a temporary measure, and we can scarcely err in believing that the period must soon arrive when all that are solvent will redeem their issues in gold and silver. Dealings abroad naturally depend on resources and prosperity at home. If the debt of our merchants has accumulated or their credit is impaired, these are fluctuations always incident to extensive or extravagant mercantile transactions. But the ultimate security of such obligations does not admit of question. They are guaranteed by the resources of a country the fruits of whose industry afford abundant means of ample liquidation, and by the evident interest of every merchant to sustain a credit hitherto high by promptly applying these means for its preservation.

I deeply regret that events have occurred which require me to ask your consideration of such serious topics. I could have wished that in making my first communication to the assembled representatives of my country I had nothing to dwell upon but the history of her unalloyed prosperity. Since it is otherwise, we can only feel more deeply the responsibility of the respective trusts that have been confided to us, and under the pressure of difficulties unite in invoking the guidance and aid of the Supreme Ruler of Nations and in laboring with zealous resolution to overcome the difficulties by which we are environed.

It is under such circumstances a high gratification to know by long experience that we act for a people to whom the truth, however unpromising, can always be spoken with safety; for the trial of whose patriotism no emergency is too severe, and who are sure never to desert a public functionary honestly laboring for the public good. It seems just that they should receive without delay any aid in their embarrassments which your deliberations can afford. Coming directly from the midst of them, and knowing the course of events in every section of our country, from you may best be learnt as well the extent and nature of these embarrassments as the most desirable measures of relief.

I am aware, however, that it is not proper to detain you at present longer than may be demanded by the special objects for which you are convened. To them, therefore, I have confined my communication; and believing it will not be your own wish now to extend your deliberations beyond them, I reserve till the usual period of your annual meeting that general information on the state of the Union which the Constitution requires me to give.

M. VAN BUREN

FIRST ANNUAL MESSAGE
December 5, 1837

The thrust of Van Buren's first message was the Independent Treasury bill which had been defeated in the earlier special session. He again urged its passage. He also spoke regretfully of the failure of his hopes for a settlement of the country's claims against Mexico. The message included a conciliatory note in his references to the dispute over the Northeastern Boundary which remained in the unsettled state the signers of the Treaty of Peace of 1783 had left it. Finally, he discussed a variety of domestic issues ranging from the Indians to the local government of the District of Columbia.

WASHINGTON, December 5, 1837.

Fellow-Citizens of the Senate and House of Representatives:

We have reason to renew the expression of our devout gratitude to the Giver of All Good for His benign protection. Our country presents on every side the evidences of that continued favor under whose auspices it has gradually risen from a few feeble and dependent colonies to a prosperous and powerful confederacy. We are blessed with domestic tranquillity and all the elements of national prosperity. The pestilence which, invading for a time some flourishing portions of the Union, interrupted the general prevalence of unusual health has happily been limited in extent and arrested in its fatal career. The industry and prudence of our citizens are gradually relieving them from the pecuniary embarrassments under which portions of them have labored; judicious legislation and the natural and boundless resources of the country have afforded wise and timely aid to private enterprise, and the activity always characteristic of our people has already in a great degree resumed its usual and profitable channels.

The condition of our foreign relations has not materially changed since the last annual message of my predecessor. We remain at peace with all nations, and no efforts on my part consistent with the preservation of our rights and the honor of the country shall be spared to maintain a position so consonant to our institutions. We have faithfully sustained the foreign policy with which the United States, under the guidance of their first President, took their stand in the family of nations—that of regulating their intercourse with other powers by the approved principles of private life; asking and according equal rights and equal privileges; rendering and demanding justice in all cases; advancing their own and discussing the pretensions of others with candor, directness, and sincerity; appealing at all times to reason, but never yielding to force nor seeking to acquire anything for themselves by its exercise.

A rigid adherence to this policy has left this Government with scarcely a claim upon its justice for injuries arising from acts committed by its authority. The most imposing and perplexing of those of the United States upon foreign governments for aggressions upon our citizens were disposed of by my predecessor. Independently of the benefits conferred upon our citizens by restoring to the mercantile community so many millions of which they had been wrongfully divested, a great service was also rendered to his country by the satisfactory adjustment of so many ancient and irritating subjects of contention; and it reflects no ordinary credit on his successful administration of public affairs that this great object was accomplished without compromising on any occasion either the honor or the peace of the nation.

With European powers no new subjects of difficulty have arisen, and those which were under discussion, although not terminated, do not present a more unfavorable aspect for the future preservation of that good understanding which it has ever been our desire to cultivate.

Of pending questions the most important is that which exists with the Government of Great Britain in respect to our northeastern boundary. It is with unfeigned regret that the people of the United States must look back upon the abortive efforts made by the Executive, for a period of more than half a century, to determine what no nation should suffer long to remain in dispute—the true line which divides its possessions from those of other powers. The nature of the settlements on the borders of the United States and of the neighboring territory was for a season such that this, perhaps, was not indispensable to a faithful performance of the duties of the Federal Government. Time has, however, changed this state of things, and has brought about a condition of affairs in which the true interests of both countries imperatively require that this question should be put at rest. It is not to be disguised that, with full confidence, often expressed, in the desire of the British Government to terminate it, we are apparently as far from its adjustment as we were at the time of signing the treaty of peace in 1783. The sole result of long-pending negotiations and a perplexing arbitration appears to be a conviction on its part that a conventional line must be adopted, from the impossibility of ascertaining the true one according to the description contained in that treaty. Without coinciding in this opinion, which is not thought to be well founded, my predecessor gave the strongest proof of the earnest desire of the United States to terminate satisfactorily this dispute by proposing the substitution of a conventional line if the consent of the States interested in the question could be obtained. To this proposition no answer has as yet been received. The attention of the British Government has, however, been urgently invited to the subject, and its reply can not,

I am confident, be much longer delayed. The general relations between Great Britain and the United States are of the most friendly character, and I am well satisfied of the sincere disposition of that Government to maintain them upon their present footing. This disposition has also, I am persuaded, become more general with the people of England than at any previous period. It is scarcely necessary to say to you how cordially it is reciprocated by the Government and people of the United States. The conviction, which must be common to all, of the injurious consequences that result from keeping open this irritating question, and the certainty that its final settlement can not be much longer deferred, will, I trust, lead to an early and satisfactory adjustment. At your last session, I laid before you the recent communications between the two Governments and between this Government and that of the State of Maine, in whose solicitude concerning a subject in which she has so deep an interest every portion of the Union participates. . . .

The aggravating circumstances connected with our claims upon Mexico and a variety of events touching the honor and integrity of our Government led my predecessor to make at the second session of the last Congress a special recommendation of the course to be pursued to obtain a speedy and final satisfaction of the injuries complained of by this Government and by our citizens. He recommended a final demand of redress, with a contingent authority to the Executive to make reprisals if that demand should be made in vain. From the proceedings of Congress on that recommendation it appeared that the opinion of both branches of the Legislature coincided with that of the Executive, that any mode of redress known to the law of nations might justifiably be used. It was obvious, too, that Congress believed with the President that another demand should be made, in order to give undeniable and satisfactory proof of our desire to avoid extremities with a neighboring power, but that there was an indisposition to vest a discretionary authority in the Executive to take redress should it unfortunately be either denied or unreasonably delayed by the Mexican Government.

So soon as the necessary documents were prepared, after entering upon the duties of my office, a special messenger was sent to Mexico to make a final demand of redress, with the documents required by the provisions of our treaty. The demand was made on the 20th of July last. The reply, which bears date the 29th of the same month, contains assurances of a desire on the part of that Government to give a prompt and explicit answer respecting each of the complaints, but that the examination of them would necessarily be deliberate; that in this examination it would be guided by the principles of public law and the obligation of treaties; that nothing should be left undone that might lead to the most speedy and equitable adjustment of our demands, and that its determination in respect to each case should be communicated through the Mexican minister here.

Since that time an envoy extraordinary and minister plenipotentiary has been accredited to this Government by that of the Mexican Republic. He brought with him assurances of a sincere desire that the pending differences between the two Governments should be terminated in a manner satisfactory to both. He was received with reciprocal assurances, and a hope was entertained that his mission would lead to a speedy, satisfactory, and final adjustment of all existing subjects of complaint. A sincere believer in the wisdom of the pacific policy by which the United States have always been governed in their intercourse with foreign nations, it was my particular desire, from the proximity of the Mexican Republic and well-known occurrences on our frontier, to be instrumental in obviating all existing difficulties with that Government and in restoring to the intercourse between the two Republics that liberal and friendly character by which they should always be distinguished. I regret, therefore, the more deeply to have found in the recent communications of that Government so little reason to hope that any future efforts of mine for the accomplishment of those desirable objects would be successful.

Although the larger number—and many of them aggravated cases of personal wrongs—have been now for years before the Mexican Government, and some of the causes of national complaint, and those of the most offensive character, admitted of immediate, simple, and satisfactory replies, it is only within a few days past that any specific communication in answer to our last demand, made five months ago, has been received from the Mexican minister. By the report of the Secretary of State herewith presented and the accompanying documents it will be seen that for not one of our public complaints has satisfaction been given or offered, that but one of the cases of personal wrong has been favorably considered, and that but four cases of both descriptions out of all those formally presented and earnestly pressed have as yet been decided upon by the Mexican Government.

Not perceiving in what manner any of the powers given to the Executive alone could be further usefully employed in bringing this unfortunate controversy to a satisfactory termination, the subject was by my predecessor referred to Congress as one calling for its interposition. In accordance with the clearly understood wishes of the Legislature, another and formal demand for satisfaction has been made upon the Mexican Government, with what success the documents now communicated will show. On a careful and deliberate examination of their contents, and considering the spirit manifested by the Mexican Government, it has become my painful duty to return the subject as it now stands to Congress, to whom it belongs to decide upon the time, the mode, and the measure of redress. Whatever may be your decision, it shall be faithfully executed, confident that it will be characterized by that moderation and justice which will, I trust, under all circumstances govern the councils of our country.

The balance in the Treasury on the 1st January, 1837, was $45,968,523. The receipts during the present year from all sources, including the amount of Treasury notes issued, are estimated at $23,499,981, constituting an aggregate of $69,468,504. Of this amount about $35,281,361 will have been expended at the end of the year on appropriations made by Congress, and the residue, amounting to $34,187,143, will be the nominal balance in the Treasury on the 1st of January next; but of that sum only $1,085,498 is considered as immediately available for and applicable to public purposes. Those portions of it which will be for some time unavailable consist chiefly of sums deposited with the States and due from the former deposit banks. The details upon this subject will be found in the annual report of the Secretary of the Treasury. The amount of Treasury notes which it will be necessary to issue during the year on account of those funds being unavailable will, it is supposed, not exceed four and a half millions. It seemed proper, in the condition of the country, to have the estimates on all subjects made as low as practicable without prejudice to any great public measures. The Departments were therefore desired to prepare their estimates accordingly, and I am happy to find that they have been able to graduate them on so economical a scale. In the great and often unexpected fluctuations to which the revenue is subjected it is not possible to compute the receipts beforehand with great certainty, but should they not differ essentially from present anticipations, and should the appropriations not much exceed the estimates, no difficulty seems likely to happen in defraying the current expenses with promptitude and fidelity.

Notwithstanding the great embarrassments which have recently occurred in commercial affairs, and the liberal indulgence which in consequence of these embarrassments has been extended to both the merchants and the banks, it is gratifying to be able to anticipate that the Treasury notes which have been issued during the present year will be redeemed and that the resources of the Treasury, without any resort to loans or increased taxes, will prove ample for defraying all charges imposed on it during 1838.

The report of the Secretary of the Treasury will afford you a more minute exposition of all matters connected with the administration of the finances during the current year—a period which for the amount of public moneys disbursed and deposited with the States, as well as the financial difficulties encountered and overcome, has few parallels in our history.

Your attention was at the last session invited to the necessity of additional legislative provisions in respect to the collection safe-keeping, and transfer of the public money. No law having been then matured, and not understanding the proceedings of Congress as intended to be final, it becomes my duties again to bring the subject to your notice.

On that occasion three modes of performing this branch of the public service were presented for consideration. These were, the creation of a national bank; the revival, with modifications, of the deposit system established by the act of the 23d of June, 1836, permitting the use of the public moneys by the banks; and the discontinuance of the use of such institutions for the purposes referred to, with suitable provisions for their accomplishment through the agency of public officers. Considering the opinions of both Houses of Congress on the first two propositions as expressed in the negative, in which I entirely concur, it is unnecessary for me again to recur to them. In respect to the last, you have had an opportunity since your adjournment not only to test still further the expediency of the measure by the continued practical operation of such parts of it as are now in force, but also to discover what should ever be sought for and regarded with the utmost deference—the opinions and wishes of the people.

The national will is the supreme law of the Republic, and on all subjects within the limits of his constitutional powers should be faithfully obeyed by the public servant. Since the measure in question was submitted to your consideration most of you have enjoyed the advantage of personal communication with your constituents. For one State only has an election been held for the Federal Government; but the early day at which it took place deprived the measure under consideration of much of the support it might otherwise have derived from the result. Local elections for State officers have, however, been held in several of the States, at which the expediency of the plan proposed by the Executive has been more or less discussed. You will, I am confident, yield to their results the respect due to every expression of the public voice. . . .

I have found no reason to change my own opinion as to the expediency of adopting the system proposed, being perfect'y satisfied that there will be neither stability nor safety either in the fiscal affairs of the Government or in the pecuniary transactions of individuals and corporations so long asa connection exists between them which, like the past, offers such strong inducements to make them the subjects of political agitation. Indeed, I am more than ever convinced of the dangers to which the free and unbiased exercise of political opinion—the only sure foundation and safeguard of republican government—would be exposed by any further increase of the already overgrown influence of corporate authorities. I can not, therefore, consistently with my views of duty, advise a renewal of a connection which circumstances have dissolved. . . .

A modification of the existing laws in respect to the prices of the public lands might also have a favorable influence on the legislation of Congress in relation to another branch of the subject. Many who have not the ability to buy at present prices settle on those lands with the hope of acquiring from their cultivation the means of purchasing under preemption laws from time to time passed by Congress. For this encroachment on the rights of the United States they excuse themselves under the plea of their own necessities; the fact that they dispossess nobody and only enter upon the waste domain: that they give additional value to the public lands in their vicinity, and their intention ultimately to pay the Government price. So much weight has from time to time been attached to these considerations that Congress have passed laws giving actual settlers on the public lands a right of preemption to the tracts occupied by them at the minimum price. These laws have in all instances been retrospective in their operation, but in a few years after their passage crowds of new settlers have been found on the public lands for similar reasons and under like expectations, who hae been indulged with the same privilege. This course of legislation tends to impair public respect for the laws of the country. Either the laws to prevent intrusion upon the public lands should be executed, or, if that should be impracticable or inexpedient, they should be modified or repealed. If the public lands are to be considered as open to be occupied by any, they should by law be thrown open to all. That which is intended in all instances to be legalized should at once be made legal, that those who are disposed to conform to the laws may enjoy at least equal privileges with those who are not. But it is not believed to be the disposition of Congress to open the public lands to occupany without regular entry and payment of the Government price, as such a course must tend to worse evils than the credit system, which it was found necessary to abolish

It would seem, therefore, to be the part of wisdom and sound policy to remove as far as practicable the causes which produce intrusions upon the public lands, and then take efficient steps to prevent them in future. Would any single measure be so effective in removing all plausible grounds for these intrusions as the graduation of price already suggested? A short period of industry and economy in any part of our country would enable the poorest citizen to accumulate the means to buy him a home at the lower prices, and leave him without apology for settling on lands not his own. If he did not under such circumstances, he would enlist no sympathy in his favor, and the laws would be readily executed without doing violence to public opinion.

A large portion of our citizens have seated themselves on the public lands without authority since the passage of the last preemption law, and now ask the enactment of another to enable them to retain the lands occupied upon payment of the minimum Government price. They ask that which has been repeatedly granted before. If the future may be judged of by the past, little harm can be done to the interests of the Treasury by yielding to their request. Upon a critical examination is found that the lands sold at the public sales since the introduction of cash payments, in 1820, have produced on an average the net revenue of only 6 cents an acre more than the minimum Government price. There is no reason to suppose that future sales will be more productive. The Government, therefore, has no adequate pecuniary interest to induce it to drive these people from the lands they occupy for the purpose of selling them to others.

Entertaining these views, I recommend the passage of a preemption law for their benefit in connection with the preparatory steps toward the graduation of the price of the public lands, and further and more effectual provisions to prevent intrusions hereafter. . . .

M. VAN BUREN

MESSAGE TO CONGRESS REQUESTING AUTHORITY TO RESTRAIN CITIZENS FROM VIOLATING TERRITORY OF NORTHERN AND SOUTHERN NEIGHBORS
January 5, 1838

Violations of Canadian and Mexican borders by U.S. private citizens prompted the Administration to seek legislation giving it greater authority to suppress and punish such invasions of "friendly and neighboring nations." An accompanying letter from the federal marshal of northern New York State illustrates the situation in the quarter.

WASHINGTON, January 5, 1838

To the Senate and House of Representatives of the United States:

Recent experience on the southern boundary of the United States and the events now daily occurring on the northern frontier have abundantly shown that the existing laws are insufficient to guard against hostile invasion from the United States of the territory of friendly and neighboring nations.

The laws in force provide sufficient penalties for the punishment of such offenses after they have been committed, and provided the parties can be found, but the Executive is powerless in many cases to prevent the commission of them, even when in possession of ample evidence of an intention on the part of evil-disposed persons to violate our laws.

Your attention is called to this defect in our legislation. It is apparent that the Executive ought to be clothed with adequate power effectually to restrain all persons without our jurisdiction from the commission of acts of this character. They tend to disturb the peace of the country and inevitably involve the Government in perplexing controversies with foreign powers. I recommend a careful revision of all the laws now in force and such additional enactments as may be necessary to vest in the Executive full power to prevent injuries being inflicted upon neighboring nations by the unauthorized and unlawful acts of citizens of the United States or of other persons who may be within our jurisdiction and subject to our control.

In illustration of these views and to show the necessity of early action on the part of Congress, I submit herewith a copy of a letter received from the marshal of the northern district of New York, who had been directed to repair to the frontier and take all authorized measures to secure the faithful execution of existing laws.

M. VAN BUREN

BUFFALO, December 28, 1837.
HIS EXCELLENCY M. VAN BUREN,

SIR: This frontier is in a state of commotion. I came to this city on the 22d instant, by direction of the United States attorney for the northern district of this State, for the purpose of serving process upon individuals suspected of violating the laws of the United States enacted with a view to maintain our neutrality. I learned on my arrival that some 200 or 300 men, mostly from the district of country adjoining this frontier and from this side of the Niagara, had congregated upon Navy Island (Upper Canada), and were there in arms, with Rensselaer van Rensselaer, of Albany, at their head as commander in chief. From that time to the present they have received constant accessions of men, munitions of war, provisions, etc., from persons residing within the States. Their whole force is now about 1,000 strong, and, as is said, are well supplied with arms, etc.

Warrants have been issued in some cases, but no arrests have as yet been effected. This expedition was got up in this city soon after McKenzie's arrival upon this side of the river, and the first company that landed upon the island were organized, partially at least, before they crossed from this side to the island.

From all that I can see and learn I am satisfied that if the Government deem it their duty to prevent supplies being furnished from this side to the army on the island, and also the augmentation of their forces from among the citizens of the States, that an armed force stationed along upon the line of the Niagara will be absolutely necessary to its accomplishment.

I have just received a communication from Colonel McNab, commanding His Majesty's forces now at Chippewa, in which he strongly urges the public authorities here to prevent supplies being furnished to the army on the island, at the same time stating that if this can be effected the whole affair could be closed without any effusion of blood.

McNab is about 2,500 strong and constantly increasing. I replied to him that I should communicate with you immediately, as also with the governor of this State, and that everything which could would be done to maintain a strict neutrality.

I learn that persons here are engaged in dislodging one or more steamboats from the ice, and, as is supposed, with a view to aid in the patriot expedition.

I am, sir, with great consideration, you obedient servant,

N. GANON,
United States Marshal, Northern District of New York

PROCLAMATIONS CALLING UPON CITIZENS TO REMAIN NEUTRAL IN CANADIAN CIVIL WAR
January 5, 1838
November 21, 1838

Americans in northern New York State were becoming involved in the insurrections which were taking place in Canada and thereby endangering relations between the United States and a "neighboring and friendly nation." Under the circumstances, Van Buren issued the Proclamation in January to warn U.S. citizens that their government will not protect them from difficulties which they may get into as a result of such interference in another territory's civil conflict. More than that, such citizens will be punished for violating U.S. neutrality laws.

The second Proclamation, issued at the end of the year in November, indicates that United States citizens were ignoring the initial warning.

By the President of the United States of America.
A PROCLAMATION

Whereas information having been received of a dangerous excitement on the northern frontier of the United States in consequence of the civil war begun in Canada, and instructions having been given to the United States officers on that frontier and applications having been made to the governors of the adjoining States to prevent any unlawful interference on the part of our citizens in the contest unfortunately commenced in the British Provinces, additional information has just been received that, notwithstanding the proclamations of the governors of the States of New York and Vermont exhorting their citizens to refrain from any unlawful acts within the territory of the United States, and notwithstanding the presence of the civil officers of the United States, who by my directions have visited the scenes of commotion with a view of impressing the citizens with a proper sense of their duty, the excitement, instead of being appeased, is every day increasing in degree; that arms and munitions of war and other supplies have been procured by the insurgents in the United States; that a military force, concisting in part, at least, of citizens of the United States, had been actually organized, had congregated at Navy Island, and were still in arms under the command of a citizen of the United States, and that they were constantly receiving accessions and aid:

Now, therefore, the end that the authority of the law may be maintained and the faith of treaties observed, I, Martin Van Buren, do most earnestly exhort all citizens of the United States who have thus violated their duties to return peaceably to their respective homes; and I hereby warn them that any persons who shall compromit the neutrality of this Government by interfering in an unlawful manner with the affairs of the neighboring British Provinces will render themselves liable to arrest and punishment under the laws of the United States, which will be rigidly enforced; and, also, that they will receive no aid of countenance from their Government, into whatever difficulties they may be thrown by the violation of the laws of their country and the territory of a neighboring and friendly nation.

Given under my hand, at the city of Washington, the 5th day of January, A.D. 1838, and the sixty-second of the Independence of the United States.

(SEAL)

M. VAN BUREN.

By the President:
JOHN FORSYTH,
    Secretary of State

By the President of the United States of America.
A PROCLAMATION.

Whereas there is too much reason to believe that citizens of the United States, in disregard to the solemn warning heretofore given to them by the proclamations issued by the Executive of the General Government and by some of the governors of the States, have combined to disturb the peace of the dominions of a neighboring and friendly nation; and

Whereas information has been given to me, derived from official and other sources, that many citizens in different parts of the United States are associated or associating for the same purpose; and

Whereas disturbances have actually broken out anew in different parts of the two Canadas; and

Whereas a hostile invasion has been made by citizens of the United States, in conjunction with Canadians and others, who, after forcibly seizing upon the property of their peaceful neighbor for the purpose of effecting their unlawful designs, are now in arms against the authorities of Canada, in perfect disregard of their obligations as American citizens and of the obligations of the Government of their country to foreign nations:

Now, therefore, I have thought it necessary and proper to issue this proclamation, calling upon every citizen of the United States neither to give countenance nor encouragement of any kind to those who have thus forfeited their claim to the protection of their country; upon those misguided or deluded persons who are engaged in them to abandon projects dangerous to their own country, fatal to those whom they profess a desire to relieve, impracticable of execution without foreign aid, which they can not rationally expect to obtain, and giving rise to imputations (however unfounded) upon the honor and good faith of their own Government; upon every officer, civil or military, and upon every citizen, by the veneration due by all freemen to the laws which they have assisted to enact for their own government, by his regard for the honor and reputation of his country, by his love of order and respect for the sacred code of laws by which national intercourse is regulated, to use every effort in his power to arrest for trial and punishment every offender against the laws providing for the performance of our obligations to the other powers of the world. And I hereby warn all those who have engaged in these criminal enterprises, if persisted in, that, whatever may be the condition to which they may be reduced, they must not expect the intereference of this Government in any form on their behalf, but will be left, reproached by every virtuous fellow-citizen, to be dealt with according to the policy and justice of that Government whose dominions they have, in defiance of the known wishes of their own Government and without the shadow of justification or excuse, nefariously invaded.

Given under my hand, at the city of Washington, the 21st day of November, A. D. 1838, and the sixty-third of the Independence (SEAL) of the United States.

M. VAN BUREN.

By the President:
JOHN FORSYTH,
Secretary of State.

SECOND ANNUAL MESSAGE
December 3, 1838

In this message Van Buren spoke cheerfully of the state of the union; the harvest had been abundant; industry was prospering; peace reigned. He noted that the year closed the first half century of federal institutions and the evidence was that it served the people best. The bulk of his report was a reiteration of his economic theories advocating the Independent Treasury. He regarded the rapid recovery of the nation without the aid of the National Bank as refutation of the opposition's arguments. Progress made by the administration to move the Indians westward was cited, although the Seminoles in Florida were an exception to this success. He also dealt with England's provocative colonial policy which threatened peace between the two nations.

WASHINGTON, December 3, 1838.

Fellow-Citizens of the Senate and House of Representatives:

I congratulate you on the favorable circumstances in the condition of our country under which you reassemble for the performance of your official duties. Though the anticipations of an abundant harvest have not everywhere been realized, yet on the whole the labors of the husbandman are rewarded with a bountiful return; industry prospers in its various channels of business and enterprise; general health again prevails through our vast diversity of climate; nothing threatens from abroad the continuance of external peace; nor has anything at home impaired the strength of those fraternal and domestic ties which constitute the only guaranty to the success and permanency of our happy Union, and which, formed in the hour of peril, have hitherto been honorably sustained through every vicissitude in our national affairs. These blessings, which evince the care and beneficence of Providence, call for our devout and fervent gratitude.

We have not less reason to be grateful for other bounties bestowed by the same munificent hand, and more exclusively our own.

The present year closes the first half century of our Federal institutions, and our system, differing from all others in the acknowledged practical and unlimited operation which it has for so long a period given to the sovereignty of the people, has now been fully tested by experience.

The Constitution devised by our forefathers as the framework and bond of that system, then untried, has become a settled form of government;

not only preserving and protecting the great principles upon which it was founded, but wonderfully promoting individual happiness and private interests. Though subject to change and entire revocation whenever deemed inadequate to all these purposes, yet such is the wisdom of its construction and so stable has been the public sentiment that it remains unaltered except in matters of detail comparatively unimportant. It has proved amply sufficient for the various emergencies incident to our condition as a nation. A formidable foreign war; agitating collisions between domestic, and in some respects rival, sovereignties; temptations to interfere in the intestine commotions of neighboring countries; the dangerous influences that arise in periods of excessive prosperity, and the antirepublican tendencies of associated wealth—these, with other trials not less formidable, have all been encountered, and thus far successfully resisted.

It was reserved for the American Union to test the advantages of a government entirely dependent on the continual exercise of the popular will, and our experience has shown that it is as beneficent in practice as it is just in theory. Each successive change made in our local institutions has contributed to extend the right of suffrage, has increased the direct influence of the mass of the community, given greater freedom to individual exertion, and restricted more and more the powers of Government; yet the intelligence, prudence, and patriotism of the people have kept pace with this augmented responsibility. In no country has education been so widely diffused. Domestic peace has nowhere so largely reigned. The close bonds of social intercourse have in no instance prevailed with such harmony over a space so vast. All forms of religion have united for the first time to diffuse charity and piety, because for the first time in the history of nations all have been totally untrammeled and absolutely free. The deepest recesses of the wilderness have been penetrated; yet instead of the rudeness in the social condition consequent upon such adventures elsewhere, numerous communities have sprung up, already unrivaled in prosperity, general intelligence, internal tranquillity, and the wisdom of their political institutions. Internal improvement, the fruit of individual enterprise, fostered by the protection of the States, has added new links to the Confederation and fresh rewards to provident industry. Doubtful questions of domestic policy have been quietly settled by mutual forbearance, and agriculture, commerce, and manufacturers minister to each other. Taxation and public debt, the burdens which bear so heavily upon all other countries, have pressed with comparative lightness upon us. Without one entangling alliance, our friendship is prized by every nation, and the rights of our citizens are everywhere respected, because they are known to be guarded by a united, sensitive, and watchful people.

To this practical operation of our institutions, so evident and successful, we owe that increased attachment to them which is among the most cheering exhibitions of popular sentiment and will prove their best security in time to come against foreign or domestic assault.

This review of the results of our institutions for half a century, without exciting a spirit of vain exultation, should serve to impress upon us the great principles from which they have sprung—constant and direct supervision by the people over every public measure, strict forbearance on the part of the Government from exercising any doubtful or disputed powers, and a cautious abstinence from all interference with concerns which properly belong and are best left to State regulations and individual enterprise.

Full information of the state of our foreign affairs having been recently on different occasions submitted to Congress, I deem it necessary now to bring to your notice only such events as have subsequently occurred or are of such importance as to require particular attention.

The most amicable dispositions continue to be exhibited by all the nations with whom the Government and citizens of the United States have an habitual intercourse. At the date of my last annual message Mexico was the only nation which could not be included in so gratifying a reference to our foreign relations.

I am happy to be now able to inform you that an advance has been made toward the adjustment of our differences with that Republic and the restoration of the customary good feeling between the two nations. This important change has been effected by conciliatory negotiations that have resulted in the conclusion of a treaty between the two Governments, which, when ratified, will refer to the arbitrament of a friendly power all the subjects of controversy between us growing out of injuries to individuals. There is at present also reason to believe that an equitable settlement of all disputed points will be attained without further difficulty or unnecessary delay, and thus authorize the free resumption of diplomatic intercourse with our sister Republic.

With respect to the northeastern boundary of the United States, no official correspondence between this Government and that of Great Britain has passed since that communicated to Congress toward the close of their last session. The offer to negotiate a convention for the appointment of a joint commission of survey and exploration I am, however, assured will be met by Her Majesty's Government in a conciliatory and friendly spirit and instructions to enable the British minister here to conclude such an arrangement will be transmitted to him without needless delay. It is hoped and expected that these instructions will be of a liberal character, and that this negotiation, if successful, will prove to be an important step toward the satisfactory and final adjustment of the controversy.

I had hoped that the respect for the laws and regard for the peace and honor of their own country which have ever characterized the citizens of the United States would have prevented any portion of them from using any means to promote insurrection in the territory of a power with which we are at peace, and with which the United States are desirous of maintaining the most friendly relations. I regret deeply, however, to be obliged to inform you that this has not been the case. Information has been given to me, derived from official and other sources, that many citizens of the United States have associated together to make hostile incursions from our territory into Canada and to aid and abet insurrection there, in violation of the obligations and laws of the United States and in open disregard of their duties as citizens. This information has been in part confirmed by by a hostile invasion actually made by citizens of the United States, in conjunction with Canadians and others, and accompanied by a forcible seizure of the property of our citizens and an application thereof to the prosecution of military operations against the authorities and peoples of Canada.

The results of these criminal assaults upon the peace and order of a neighboring country have been, as was to be expected, fatally destructive to the misguided or deluded persons engaged in them and highly injurious to those in whose behalf they are professed to have been undertaken. The authorities in Canada, from intelligence received of such intended movements among our citizens, have felt themselves obliged to take precautionary measures against them; have actually embodied the militia and assumed an attitude to repel the invasion to which they believed the colonies were exposed from the United States. A state of feeling on both sides of the frontier has thus been produced which called for prompt and vigorous interference. If an insurrection existed in Canada, the amicable dispositions of the United States toward Great Britain, as well as their duty to themselves, would lead them to maintain a strict neutrality and to restrain their citizens from all violations of the laws which have been passed for its enforcement. But this Government recognizes a still higher obligation to repress all attempts on the part of its citizens to disturb the peace of a country where order prevails or has been reestablished. Depredations by our citizens upon nations at peace with the United States, or combinations for committing them, have at all times been regarded by the American Government and people with the greatest abhorrence. Military incursions by our citizens into countries so situated, and the commission of acts of violence on the members thereof, in order to effect a change in their government, or under any pretext whatever, have from the commencement of our Government been held equally criminal on the part of those engaged in them, and as much deserving of punishment as would be the disturbance of the public peace by the perpetration of similar acts within our own territory. . . .

When we call to mind the recent and extreme embarrassments produced by excessive issues of bank paper, aggravted by the unforeseen withdrawal of much foreign capital and the inevitable derangement arising from the distribution of the surplus revenue among the States as required by Congress, and consider the heavy expenses incurred by the removal of Indian tribes, by the military operations in Florida, and on account of the unusually large appropriations made at the last two annual sessions of Congress for other objects, we have striking evidence in the present efficient state of our finances of the abundant resources of the country to fulfill all its obligations. Nor is it less gratifying to find that the general business of the community, deeply affected as it has been, is reviving with additional vigor, chastened by the lessons of the past and animated by the hopes of the future. By the curtailment of paper issues, by curbing the sanguine and adventurous spirit of speculation, and by the honorable application of all available means to the fulfillment of obligations, confidence has been restored both at home and abroad, and ease and facility secured to all the operations of trade.

The agency of the Government in producing these results has been as efficient as its powers and means permitted. By withholding from the States the deposit of the fourth installment, and leaving several millions at long credits with the banks, principally in one section of the country, and more immediately beneficial to it, and at the same time aiding the banks and commercial communities in other sections by postponing the payment of bonds for duties to the amount of between four and five millions of dollars; by an issue of Treasury notes as a means to enable the Government to meet the consequences of their indulgences but affording at the same time facilities for remittance and exchange; and by steadily declining to employ as general depositories of the public revenues, or receive the notes of, all banks which refused to redeem them with specie— by these measures, aided by the favorable action of some of the banks and by the support and cooperation of a large portion of the community, we have witnessed an early resumption of specie payments in our great commercial capital, promptly followed in almost every part of the United States. This result has been alike salutary to the true interests of agriculture, commerce, and manufactures; to public morals, respect for the laws, and that confidence between man and man which is so essential in all our social relations.

The contrast between the suspension of 1814 and that of 1837 is most striking. The short duration of the latter, the prompt restoration of business, the evident benefits resulting from an adherence by the Government to the constitutional standard of value instead of sanctioning the suspension by the receipt of irredeemable paper, and the advantages derived from the large amount of specie introduced into the country previous to 1837 afford a valuable illustration of the true policy of the Government in such a crisis. Nor can the comparison fail to remove the impression that a national bank is necessary in such emergencies. Not only where specie payments resumed without its aid, but exchanges have also been more rapidly restored than when it existed, thereby showing that private capital, enterprise, and prudence are fully adequate to these ends. On all these points experience seems to have confirmed the views heretofore submitted to Congress. We have been saved the moritification of seeing the distresses of the community for the third time seized on to fasten upon the country so dangerous an institution, and we may also hope that the business of individuals will hereafter be relieved from the injurious effects of a continued agitation of that disturbing subject. The limited influence of a national bank in averting derangement in the exchanges of the country or in compelling the resumption of specie payments is now not less apparent than its tendency to increase inordinate speculation by sudden expansions and contractions; its disposition to create panic and embarrassment for the promotion of its own designs; its interference with, politics, and its far greater power for evil than for good, either in regard to the local institutions or the operations of Government itself. What was in these respects but apprehension or opinion when a national bank was first established now stands confirmed by humiliating experience. The scenes through which we have passed conclusively prove how little our commerce, agriculture, manufactures, or finances require such an institution, and what dangers are attendant on its power—a power, I trust, never to be conferred by the American people upon their Government, and still less upon individuals—not responsible to them for its unavoidable abuses. . . .

It affords me sincere pleasure to be able to apprise you of the entire removal of the Cherokee Nation of Indians to their new homes west of the Mississippi. The measures authorized by Congress at its last session with a view to the long-standing controversy with them, have had the happiest effects. By an agreement concluded with them by the commanding general in that country, who has performed the duties assigned to him on the occasion with commendable energy and humanity, their removal has been principally under the conduct of their own chiefs, and they have emigrated without any apparent reluctance.

The successful accomplishment of this important object, the removal also of the entire Creek Nation, with the exception of a small number of fugitives amongst the Seminoles in Florida, the progress already made toward a speedy completion of the removal of the Chickasaws, the Choctaws, the Pottawatamies, the Ottawas, and the Chippewas, with the extensive purchases of Indian lands during the present year, have rendered the speedy and successful result of the long-established policy of the Government upon the subject of Indian affairs entirely certain. The occasion is therefore deemed a proper one to place this policy in such a point of view as will exonerate the Government of the United States from the undeserved reproach which has been cast upon it through several successive Administrations. That a mixed occupancy of the same territory of the white and red man is incompatible with the safety or happiness of either is a position in respect to which there has long since ceased to be room for a difference of opinion. Reason and experience have alike demonstrated its impracticability. The bitter fruits of every attempt heretofore to overcome the barriers interposed by nature have only been destruction, both physical and moral, to the Indian, dangerous conflicts of authority between the Federal and State Governments, and detriment to the individual prosperity of the citizen as well as to the general improvement of the country. The remedial policy, the principles of which were settled more than thirty years ago under the Administration of Mr. Jefferson, consists in an extinction, for a fair consideration, of the title to all the lands still occupied by the Indians within the States and Territories of the United States; their removal to a country west of the Mississippi much more extensive and better adapted to their condition than that on which they then resided; the guarantee to them by the United States of their exclusive possession of that country forever, exempt from all intrusions by white men, with ample provisions for their security against external violence and internal dissensions, and the extension to them of suitable facilities for their advancement in civilization. This has not been the policy of particular Administrations only, but of each in succession since the first attempt to carry it out under that of Mr. Monroe. All have labored for its accomplishments, only with different degrees of success. The manner of its execution has, it is true, from time to time given rise to conflicts of opinion and unjust imputations; but in respect to the wisdom and necessity of the policy itself there has not from the beginning existed a doubt in the mind of any calm, judicious, disinterested friend of the Indian race accustomed to reflection and enlightened by experience.

Occupying the double character of contractor on its own account and guardian for the parties contracted with, it was hardly to be expected that the dealings of the Federal Government with the Indian tribes would escape misrepresentation. That there occurred in the early settlement of this country, as in all others where the civilized race has succeeded to the possessions of the savage, instances of oppression and fraud on the part of the former there is too much reason to believe. No such offenses can, however, be justly charged upon this Government since it became free to pursue its own course. Its dealings with the Indian tribes have been just and friendly throughout; its efforts for their civilization constant, and directed by the best feelings of humanity; its watchfulness in protecting them from individual frauds unremitting; its forbearance under the keenest provocations, the deepest injuries, and the most flagrant outrages may challenge at least a comparison with any nation, ancient or modern, in similar circumstances; and if in future times a powerful, civilized, and happy nation of Indians shall be found to exist within the limits of this northern continent it will be owing to the consummation of that policy which has been so unjustly assailed. Only a very brief reference to facts in confirmation of this assertion can in this form be given, and you are therefore necessarily referred to the report of the Secretary of War for further details. To the Cherokees, whose case has perhaps excited the greatest share of attention and sympathy, the United States have granted in fee, with a perpetual guaranty of exclusive and peaceable possession, 13,554,135 acres of land on the west side of the Mississippi, eligibly situated, in a healthy climate, and in all respects better suited to their condition than the country they have left, in exchange for only 9,492,160 acres on the east side of the same river. The United States have in addition stipulated to pay them $5,600,000 for their interest in and improvements on the lands thus relinquished, and $1,160,000 for subsistence and other beneficial purposes, thereby putting it in their power to become one of the most wealthy and independent separate communities of the same extent in the world.

By the treaties made and ratified with the Miamies, the Chippewas, the Sioux, the Sacs and Foxes, and the Winnebagoes during the last year the Indian title to 18,458,000 acres has been extinguished. These purchases have been much more extensive than those of any previous year, and have, with other Indian expenses, borne very heavily upon the Treasury. They leave, however, but a small quantity of unbought Indian lands within the States and Territories, and the Legislature and Executive were equally sensible of the propriety of a final and more speedy extinction of Indian titles within those limits. The treaties, which were with a single exception made in pursuance of previous appropriations for defraying the expenses, have subsequently been ratified by the Senate, and received the sanction of Congress by the appropriations necessary to carry them into effect. Of the terms upon which these important negotiations were concluded I can speak from direct knowledge, and I feel no difficulty in affirming that the interest of the Indians in the extensive territory embraced by them is to be paid for at its fair value, and that no more favorable terms have been granted to the United States than would have been reasonably expected in a negotiation with civilized men fully capable of appreciating and protecting their own rights. For the Indian title to 116,349,897 acres acquired since the 4th of March, 1829, the United States have paid $72,560,056 in permanent annutities, lands, reservations for Indians, expenses of removal and subsistence, merchandise, mechanical and agricultural establishments and implements. When the heavy expenses incurred by the United States and the circumstance that so large a portion of the entire territory will be forever unsalable are considered, and this price is compared with that for which the United States sell their own lands, no one can doubt that justice has been done to the Indians in these purchases also. Certain it is that the transactions of the Federal Government with the Indians have been uniformly characterized by a sincere and paramount desire to promote their welfare; and it must be a source of the highest gratification to every friend to justice and humanity to learn that nothwithstanding the obstructions from time to time thrown in its way and the difficulties which have arisen from the peculiar and impracticable nature of the Indian character, the wise, humane, and undeviating policy of the Government in this the most difficult of all our relations, foreign or domestic, has at length been justified to the world in its near approach to a happy and certain consummation.

The condition of the tribes which occupy the country set apart for them in the West is highly prosperous, and encourages the hope of their early civilization. They have for the most part abandoned the hunter state and turned their attention to agricultural pursuits. All those who have been established for any length of time in that fertile region maintain themselves by their own industry. There are among them traders of no inconsiderable capital, and planters exporting cotton to some extent, but the greater number are small agriculturists, living in comfort upon the produce of their farms. The recent emigrants, although they have in some instances removed reluctantly, have readily acquiesced in their un-avoidable destiny. They have found at once a recompense for past suffer-ings and an incentive to industrious habits in the abundance and comforts around them. There is reason to believe that all these tribes are friendly in their feelings toward the United States; and it is to be hoped that the acquisition of individual wealth, the pursuits of agriculture, and habits of industry will gradually subdue their warlike propensities and incline them to maintain peace among themselves. To effect this desirable object the attention of Congress is solicited to the measures recommended by the Secretary of War for their future government and protection, as well from each other as from the hostility of the warlike tribes around them and the intrusions of the whites. The policy of the Government has given them a permanent home and guaranteed to them its peaceful and undisturbed possession. It only remains to give them a government and laws which will encourage industry and secure to them the rewards of their exer-tions. The importance of some form of government can not be too much insisted upon. The earliest effects will be to diminish the causes and occasions for hostilities among the tribes, to inspire an interest in the observance of laws to which they will have themselves assented, and to multiply the securities of property and the motives for self-improvement. Intimately connected with this subject is the establishment of the military defenses recommended by the Secretary of War, which have been already referred to. Without them the Government will be powerless to redeem its pledge of protection to the emigrating Indians against the numerous warlike tribes that surround them and to provide for the safety of the frontier settlers of the bordering States.

The case of the Seminoles constitutes at present the only exception to the successful efforts of the Government to remove the Indians to the homes assigned them west of the Mississippi. Four hundred of this tribe emigrated in 1836 and 1,500 in 1837 and 1838, leaving in the country, it is supposed, about 2,000 Indians. The continued treacherous conduct of these people; the savage and unprovoked murders they have lately committed, butchering whole families of the settlers of the Territory with-out distinction of age or sex, and making their way into the very center and heart of the country, so that no part of it is free from their ravages; their frequent attacks on the light-houses along that dangerous coast, and the barbarity with which they have murdered the passengers and crews of such vessels as have been wrecked upon the reefs and keys which border the Gulf, leave the Government no alternative but to continue the military operations against them until they are totally expelled from Flor-ida. There are other motives which would urge the Government to pursue this course toward the Seminoles. The United States have fulfilled in good faith all their treaty stipulations with the Indian tribes, and have in every other instance insisted upon a like performance of their obligations. To relax from this salutary rule because the Seminoles have maintained themselves so long in the territory they had relinquished, and in defiance of their frequent and solemn engagements still continue to wage a ruthless war against the United States, would not only evince a want of constancy on our part, but be of evil example in our intercourse with other tribes. Experience has shown that but little is to be gained by the march of armies through a country so intersected with inaccessible swamps and marshes, and which, from the fatal character of the climate, must be abandoned at the end of the winter. I recommend, therefore, to your attention the plan submitted by the Secretary of War in the accompanying report, for the permanent occupation of the portion of the Territory freed from the Indians and the more efficient protection of the people of Florida from their inhuman warfare. . . .

M. VAN BUREN.

MESSAGE TO CONGRESS ON
NORTHEASTERN BOUNDARY DISPUTE
February 26, 1839

A series of trespasses by Canadian authorities, originating in the disputed Northeastern Boundary between Maine and Canada, culminated late in 1838 in the seizure of an agent of Maine who had been sent to investigate reports that bands of trespassers from New Brunswick were cutting timber in the Aroostook region. As soon as information of the border trouble reached Washington, Van Buren—after negotiations between the Secretary of State and the British minister failed—transmitted the correspondence to Congress with a message sustaining the action of Maine. While expressing hope that mutual exercise of jurisdiction over the disputed territory by the authorities of Maine and the Canadian Province would be continued pending arbitration, which had been agreed upon years back, he sought authority from Congress to call out 50,000 volunteers to aid Maine if he deemed it necessary. The measure reached the Senate on March 2 and was passed the same day.

To the Senate and House of Representatives:

I lay before Congress several dispatches from his excellency the governor of Maine, with inclosures, communicating certain proceedings of the legislature of that State, and a copy of the reply of the Secretary of State, made by my direction, together with a note from H. S. Fox, esq., envoy, extraordinary and minister plenipotentiary of Great Britain, with the answer of the Secretary of State to the same.

It will appear from those documents that a numerous band of lawless and desperate men, chiefly from the adjoining British Provinces, but without the authority of sanction of the provincial government, had trespassed upon that portion of the territory in dispute between the United States and Great Britain which is watered by the river Aroostook and claimed to belong to the State of Maine, and that they had committed extensive depredations there by cutting and destroying a very large quanity of timber. It will further appear that the governor of Maine, having been officially apprised of the circumstance, had communicated it to the legislature with a recommendation of such provisions in addition to those already existing by law as would enable him to arrest the course of said depredations, disperse the trespassers, and secure the timber which they were about carrying away; that, in compliance with a resolve of the legislature passed in pursuance of his recommendation, his excellency had dispatched the land agent of the State, with a force deemed adequate to that purpose, to the scene of the alleged depredations, who, after accomplishing a part of his duty, was seized by a band of the treaspassers at a house claimed to be within the jurisdiction of Maine, whither he had repaired for the purpose of meeting and consulting with the land agent of the Province of New Brunswick, and conveyed as a prisoner to Frederickton, in that Province, together with two other citizens of the State who were assisting him in the discharge of his duty.

It will also appear that the governor and legislature of Maine, satisfied that the trespassers had acted in defiance of the laws of both countries, learning that they were in possession of arms, and anticipating (correctly, as the result has proved) that persons of their reckless and desperate character would set at naught the authority of the magistrates without the aid of a strong force, had authorized the sheriff and the officer appointed in the place of the land agent to employ, at the expense of the State, an armed posse, who had proceeded to the scene of these depreda-

In the correspondence between the governor of Maine and Sir John Harvey, lieutenant governor of the Province of New Brunswick, which has grown out of these occurrences and is likewise herewith communicated, the former is requested to recall the armed party advanced into the disputed territory for the arrest of trespassers, and is informed that a strong body of British troops is to be held in readiness to support and protect the authority and subjects of Great Britain in said territory. In answer to that request the provincial governor is informed of the determination of the State of Maine to support the land agent and his party in the performance of their duty, and the same determination, for the execution of which provision is made by a resolve of the State legislature, is communicated by the governor to the General Government.

The lieutenant-governor of New Brunswick, in calling upon the governor of Maine for the recall of the land agent and his party from the disputed territory, and the British minister, in making a similar demand upon the Government of the United States, proceed upon the assumption that an agreement exists between the two nations conceding to Great Britain, until the final settlement of the boundary question, exclusive possession of and jurisdiction over the territory in dispute. The important bearing which such an agreement, if it existed, would have upon the condition and interests of the parties, and the influence it might have upon the adjustment of the dispute, are too obvious to allow the error upon which this assumption seems to rest to pass for a moment without correction. The answer of the Secretary of State to Mr. Fox's note will show the ground taken by the Government of the United States upon this point. It is believed that all the correspondence which has passed between the two Governments upon this subject has already been communicated to Congress and is now on their files. An abstract of it, however, hastily prepared, accompanies this communication. It is possible that in thus abridging a voluminous correspondence, commencing in 1825 and continuing to a very recent period, a portion may have been accidentally overlooked; but it is believed that nothing has taken place which would materially change the aspect of the question as therein presented. Instead of sustaining the assumption of the British functionaries, that correspondence disproves the existence of any such agreement. It shows that the two Governments have differed not only in regard to the main question of title to the territory in dispute, but with reference also to the right of jurisdiction and the fact of the actual exercise of it in different portions thereof.

Always aiming at an amicable adjustment of the dispute, both parties have entertained and repeatedly urged upon each other a desire that each should exercise its rights, whatever it considered them to be, in such a manner as to avoid collision and allay to the greatest practicable extent the excitement likely to grow out of the controversy. It was in pursuance of such an understanding that Maine and Massachusetts, upon the remonstrance of Great Britain, desisted from making sales of lands, and the General Government from the construction of a projected military road in a portion of the territory of which they claimed to have enjoyed the exclusive possession; and that Great Britain on her part, in deference to a similar remonstrance from the United States, suspended the issue of licenses to cut timber in the territory in controversy and also the survey and location of a railroad through a section of country over which she also claimed to have exercised exclusive jurisdiction.

The State of Maine had a right to arrest the depredations complained of. It belonged to her to judge of the exigency of the occasion calling for her interference, and it is presumed that had the lieutenant-governor of New Brunswick been correctly advised of the nature of the proceedings of the State of Maine he would not have regarded the transaction as requiring on his part any resort to force. Each party claiming a right to the territory, and hence to the exclusive jurisdiction over it, it is manifest that to prevent the destruction of the timber by trespassers, acting against the authority of both, and at the same time avoid forcible collision between the contiguous governments during the pendency of negotiations concerning the title, resort must be had to the mutual exercise of jurisdiction in such extreme cases or to an amicable and temporary arrangement as to the limits within which it should be exercised by each party. The understanding supposed to exist between the United States and Great Britain has been found heretofore sufficient for that purpose, and I believe will prove so hereafter if the parties on the frontier directly interested in the question are respectively governed by a just spirit of conciliation and forbearance. If it shall be found, as there is now reason to apprehend, that there is, in the modes of construing that understanding by the two Governments, a difference not to be reconciled, I shall not hesitate to propose to Her Britannic Majesty's Government a distinct arrangement for the temporary and mutual exercise of jurisdiction by means of which similar difficulties may in future be prevented.

But between an effort on the part of Maine to preserve the property in dispute from destruction by intruders and a military occupation by that State of the territory with a view to hold it by force while the settlement is a subject of negotiation between the two Governments there is an essential difference, as well in respect to the position of the State as to the duties of the General Government. In a letter addressed by the Secretary of State to the governor of Maine on the 1st of March last, giving a detailed statement of the steps which had been taken by the Federal Government to bring the controversy to a termination, and designed to apprise the governor of that State of the views of the Federal Executive in respect to the future, it was stated that while the obligations of the Federal Government to do all in its powers to effect the settlement of the boundary question were fully recognized, it had, in the event of being unable to do so specifically by mutual consent, no other means to accomplish that object amicably than by another arbitration, or by a commission, with an umpire, in the nature of an arbitration; and that in the event of all other measures failing the President would feel it his duty to submit another proposition to the Government of Great Britain to refer the decision of the question to a third power. These are still my views upon the subject, and until this step shall have been taken I can not think it proper to invoke the attention of Congress to other than amicable means for the settlement of the controversy, or to cause the military power of the Federal Government to be brought in aid of the State of Maine in any attempt to effect that object by a resort to force.

On the other hand, if the authorities of New Brunswick should attempt to enforce the claim of exclusive jurisdiction set up by them by means of a military occupation on their part of the disputed territory, I shall feel myself bound to consider the contingency provided by the Constitution as having occurred, on the happening of which a State has the right to call for the aid of the Federal Government to repel invasion.

I have expressed to the British minister near this Government a confident expectation that the agents of the State of Maine, who have been arrested under an obvious misapprehension of the object of their mission, will be promptly released, and to the governor of Maine that a similar course will be pursued in regard to the agents of the Province of New Brunswick. I have also recommended that any militia that may have been brought together by the State of Maine from an apprehension of a collision with the government or people of the British Province will be voluntarily and peaceably disbanded.

I can not allow myself to doubt that the results anticipated from these representations will be seasonably realized. The parties more immediately interested can not but perceive that an appeal to arms under existing circumstances will not only prove fatal to their present interests, but would postpone, if not defeat, the attainment of the main objects which they have in view. The very incidents which have recently occurred will necessarily awaken the Gvernments to the importance of promptly adjusting a dispute by which it is now made manifest that the peace of the two nations is daily and imminently endangered. This expectation is further warranted by the general forbearance which has hitherto characterized the conduct of the Government and people on both sides of the line. In the uniform patriotism of Maine, her attachment to the Union, her respect for the wishes of the people of her sister States (of whose interest in her welfare she can not be unconscious), and in the solicitude felt by the country at large for the preservation of peace with our neighbors, we have a strong guaranty that she will not disregard the request that has been made of her.

As, however, the session of Congress is about to terminate and the agency of the Executive may become necessary during the recess, it is important that the attention of the Legislature should be drawn to the consideration of such measures as may be calculated to obviate the necessity of a call for an extra session. With that view I have thought it my duty to lay the whole matter before you and to invite such action thereon as you may think the occasion requires.

M. VAN BUREN.

THIRD ANNUAL MESSAGE
December 2, 1839

The thrust of this message was again an attack on the paper banking system and a plea for the Independent Treasury. He was particularly concerned over the emergence of a national public debt, and therefore urged "retrenchment and reform" by cutting down both public and private expenditures, paying up debts, and, above all, reforming the banking system.

WASHINGTON, December 2, 1839.

Fellow-Citizens of the Senate and House of Representatives:

I regret that I can not on this occasion congratulate you that the past year has been one of unalloyed prosperity. The ravages of fire and disease have painfully afflicted otherwise flourishing portions of our country, and serious embarrassments yet derange the trade of many of our cities. But notwithstanding these adverse circumstances, that general prosperity which has been heretofore so bountifully bestowed upon us by the Author of All Good still continues to call for our warmest gratitude. Especially have we reason to rejoice in the exuberant harvests which have lavishly recompensed well-directed industry and given to it that sure reward which is vainly sought in visionary speculations. I can not, indeed, view without peculiar satisfaction the evidences afforded by the past season of the benefits that spring from the steady devotion of the husbandman to his honorable pursuit. No means of individual comfort is more certain and no source of national prosperity is so sure. Nothing can compensate a people for a dependence upon others for the bread they eat, and that cheerful abundance on which the happiness of everyone so much depends is to be looked for nowhere with such sure reliance as in the industry of the agriculturist and the bounties of the earth.

With foreign countries our relations exhibit the same favorable aspect which was presented in my last annual message, and afford continued proof of the wisdom of the pacific, just, and forbearing policy adopted by the first Administration of the Federal Government and pursued by its successors. The extraordinary powers vested in me by an act of Congress for the defense of the country in an emergency, considered so far probable as to require that the Executive should possess ample means to meet it, have not been exerted. They have therefore been attended with no other result than to increase, by the confidence thus reposed in me, my obligations to maintain with religious exactness the cardinal principles that govern our intercourse with other nations. Happily, in our pending

questions with Great Britain, out of which this unusual grant of authority arose, nothing has occurred to require its exertion, and as it is about
to return to the Legislature I trust that no future necessity may call for
its exercise by them or its delegation to another Department of the
Government.

For the settlement of our northeastern boundary the proposition promised by Great Britain for a commission of exploration and survey has been
received, and a counter project, including also a provision for the certain
and final adjustment of the limits in dispute, is now before the British
Government for its consideration. A just regard to the delicate state of
this question and a proper respect for the natural impatience of the State
of Maine, not less than a conviction that the negotiation has been already
protracted longer than is prudent on the part of either Government, have
led me to believe that the present favorable moment should on no account
be suffered to pass without putting the question forever at rest. I feel
confident that the Government of Her Britannic Majesty will take the
same view of this subject, as I am persuaded it is governed by desires
equally strong and sincere for the amicable termination of the controversy. . . .

The creation in time of peace of a debt likely to become permanent
is an evil for which there is no equivalent. The rapidity with which many
of the States are apparently approaching to this condition admonishes us
of our own duties in a manner too impressive to be disregarded. One,
not the least important, is to keep the Federal Government always in a
condition to discharge with ease and vigor its highest functions should
their exercise be required by any sudden conjuncture of public affairs—a
condition to which we are always exposed and which may occur when it
is least expected. To this end it is indispensable that its finances should
be untrammeled and its resources as far as practicable unencumbered. No
circumstance could present greater obstacles to the accomplishment of
these vitally important objects than the creation of an onerous national
debt. Our own experience and also that of other nations have demonstrated the unavoidable and fearful rapidity with which a public debt is
increased when the Government has once surrendered itself to the ruinous
practice of supplying its supposed necessities by new loans. The struggle,
therefore, on our part to be successful must be made at the threshold.
To make our efforts effective, severe economy is necessary. This is the
surest provision for the national welfare, and it is at the same time the
best preservative of the principles on which our institutions rest. Simplic-
ity and economy in the affairs of state have never failed to chasten and
invigorate republican principles, while these have been as surely subverted
by national prodigality, under whatever specious pretexts it may have been
introduced or fostered. . . .

The continued agitation of the question relative to the best mode of
keeping and disbursing the public money still injuriously affects the business of the country. The suspension of specie payments in 1837 rendered

the use of deposit banks as prescribed by the act of 1836 a source rather of embarrassment than aid, and of necessity placed the custody of most of the public money afterwards collected in charge of the public officers. The new securities for its safety which this required were a principal cause of my convening an extra session of Congress, but in consequence of a disagreement between the two Houses neither then nor at any subsequent period has there been any legislation on the subject. The effort made at the last session to obtain the authority of Congress to punish the use of public money for private purposes as a crime—a measure attended under other governments with signal advantage—was also unsuccessful, from diversities of opinion in that body, notwithstanding the anxiety doubtless felt by it to afford every practicable security. The result of this is still to leave the custody of the public money without those safeguards which have been for several years earnestly desired by the Executive, and as the remedy is only to be found in the action of the Legislature it imposes on me the duty of again submitting to you the propriety of passing a law providing for the safe-keeping of the public moneys, and especially to ask that its use for private purposes by any officers intrusted with it may be declared to be a felony, punishable with penalties proportioned to the magnitude of the offense. . . .

I have heretofore assigned to Congress my reasons for believing that the establishment of an independent National Treasury, as contemplated by the Constitution, is necessary to the safe action of the Federal Government. The suspension of specie payments in 1837 by the banks having the custody of the public money showed in so alarming a degree our dependence on those institutions for the performance of duties required by law that I then recommended the entire dissolution of that connection. This recommendation has been subjected, as I desired it should be, to severe scrutiny and animated discussion, and I allow myself to believe that notwithstanding the natural diversities of opinion which may be anticipated on all subjects involving such important considerations, it has secured in its favor as general a concurrence of public sentiment as could be expected on one of such magnitude.

Recent events have also continued to develop new objections to such a connection. Seldom is any bank, under the existing system and practice, able to meet on demand all its liabilities for deposits and notes in circulation. It maintains specie payments and transacts a profitable business only by the confidence of the public in its solvency, and whenever this is destroyed the demands of its depositors and note holders, pressed more rapidly than it can make collections from its debtors, force it to stop payment. This loss of confidence, with its consequences, occurred in 1837, and afforded the apology of the banks for their suspension. The public then acquiesced in the validity of the excuse, and while the State legislatures did not exact from them their forfeited charters, Congress, in accordance with the recommendation of the Executive, allowed them time to pay over the public money they held, although compelled to issue Treasury notes to supply the deficiency thus created.

It now appears that there are other motives than a want of public confidence under which the banks seek to justify themselves in a refusal to meet their obligations. Scarcely were the country and Government relieved in a degree from the difficulties occasioned by the general suspension of 1837 when a partial one, occurring within thirty months of the former, produced new and serious embarrassments, though it had no palliation in such circumstances as were alleged in justification of that which had previously taken place. There was nothing in the condition of the country to endanger a well-managed banking institution; commerce was deranged by no foreign war; every branch of manufacturing industry was crowned with rich rewards, and the more than usual abundance of our harvests, after supplying our domestic wants, had left our granaries and storehouses filled with a surplus for exportation. It is in the midst of this that an irredeemable and depreciated paper currency is entailed upon the people by a large portion of the banks. They are not driven to it by the exhibition of a loss of public confidence or of a sudden pressure from their depositors or note holders, but they excuse themselves by alleging that the current of business and exchange with foreign countries, which draws the precious metals from their vaults, would require in order to meet it a larger curtailment of their loans to a comparatively small portion of the community than it will be convenient for them to bear or perhaps safe for the banks to exact. The plea has ceased to be one of necessity. Convenience and policy are now deemed sufficient to warrant these institutions in disregarding their solemn obligations. Such conduct is not merely an injury to individual creditors, but it is a wrong to the whole community, from whose liberality they hold most valuable privileges, whose rights they violate, whose business they derange, and the value of whose property they render unstable and insecure. It must be evident that this new ground for bank suspensions, in reference to which their action is not only disconnected with, but wholly independent of, that of the public, gives a character to their suspensions more alarming than any which they exhibited before, and greatly increases the impropriety of relying on the banks in the transactions of the Government.

A large and highly respectable portion of our banking institutions are, it affords me unfeigned pleasure to state, exempted from all blame on account of this second delinquency. They have, to their great credit, not only continued to meet their engagements, but have even repudiated the grounds of suspension now resorted to. It is only by such a course that the confidence and good will of the community can be preserved, and in the sequel the best interests of the institutions themselves promoted.

New dangers to the banks are also daily disclosed from the extension of that system of extravagant credit of which they are the pillars. Formerly our foreign commerce was principally founded on an exchange of commodities, including the precious metals, and leaving in its transactions but little foreign debt. Such is not now the case. Aided by the facilities afforded by the banks, mere credit has become too commonly the basis of trade. Many of the banks themselves, not content with largely stimulating their system among others, have usurped the business, while they impair the stability, of the mercantile community; they have become borrowers instead of lenders; they establish their agencies abroad; they deal largely in stocks and merchandise; they encourage the issue of State securities until the foreign market is glutted with them; and, unsatisfied with the legitimate use of their own capital and the exercise of their lawful privileges, they raise by large loans additional means for every variety of speculation. The disasters attendant on this deviation from the former course of business in this country are now shared alike by banks and individuals to an extent of which there is perhaps no previous example in the annals of our country. So long as a willingness of the foreign lender and a sufficient export of our productions to meet any necessary partial payments leave the flow of credit undisturbed all appears to be prosperous, but as soon as it is checked by any hestiation abroad or by an inability to make payment there in our productions the evils of the system are disclosed. The paper currency, which might serve for domestic purposes, is useless to pay the debt due in Europe. Gold and silver are therefore drawn in exchange for their notes from the banks. To keep up their supply of coin these institutions are obliged to call upon their own debtors, who pay them principally in their own notes, which are as unavailable to them as they are to the merchants to meet the foreign demand. The calls of the banks, therefore, in such emergencies of necessity exceed that demand, and produce a corresponding curtailment of their accommodations and of the currency at the very moment when the state of trade renders it most inconvenient to be borne. The intensity of this pressure on the community is in proportion to the previous liberality of credit and consequent expansion of the currency. Forced sales of property are made at the time when the means of purchasing are most reduced, and the worst calamities to individuals are only at last arrested by an open violation of their obligations by the banks—a refusal to pay specie for their notes and an imposition upon the community of a fluctuating and depreciated currency.

These consequences are inherent in the present system. They are not influenced by the banks being large or small, created by National or State Governments. They are the results of the irresistible laws of trade or credit. In the recent events, which have so strikingly illustrated the certain effects of these laws, we have seen the bank of the largest capital in the Union, established under a national charter, and lately strengthened, as we were authoritatively informed, by exchanging that for a State charter with new and unusual privileges—in a condition, too, as it was said, of entire soundness and great prosperity—not merely unable to resist these effects, but the first to yield to them.

Nor is it to be overlooked that there exists a chain of necessary dependence among these institutions which obliges them to a great extent to follow the course of others, notwithstanding its injustice to their own immediate creditors or injury to the particular community in which they are placed. This dependence of a bank, which is in proportion to the extent of its debts for circulation and deposits, is not merely on others in its own vicinity, but on all those which connect it with the center of trade. Distant banks may fail without seriously affecting those in our principal commercial cities, but the failure of the latter is felt at the extremities of the Union. The suspension at New York in 1837 was everywhere, with very few exceptions, followed as soon as it was known. That recently at Philadelphia immediately affected the banks of the South and West in a similar manner. This dependence of our whole banking system on the institutions in a few large cities is not found in the laws of their organization, but in those of trade and exchange. The banks at that center, to which currency flows and where it is required in payments for merchandise, hold the power of controlling those in regions whence it comes, while the latter possess no means of restraining them; so that the value of individual property and the prosperity of trade through the whole interior of the country are made to depend on the good or bad management of the banking institutions in the great seats of trade on the seaboard.

But this chain of dependence does not stop here. It does not terminate at Philadelphia or New York. It reaches across the ocean and ends in London, the center of the credit system. The same laws of trade which give to the banks in our principal cities power over the whole banking system of the United States subject the former, in their turn, to the money power in Great Britain. It is not denied that the suspension of the New York banks in 1837, which was followed in quick succession throughout the Union, was produced by an application of that power, and it is now alleged, in extenuation of the present condition of so large a portion of our banks, that their embarrassments have arisen from the same cause.

From this influence they can not now entirely escape, for it has its origin in the credit currencies of the two countries; it is strengthened by the current of trade and exchange which centers in London, and is rendered almost irresistible by the large debts contracted there by our merchants, our banks, and our States. It is thus that an introduction of a new bank into the most distant of our villages places the business of that village within the influence of the money power in England; it is thus that every new debt which we contract in that country seriously affects our own currency and extends over the pursuits of our citizens its powerful influence. We can not escape from this by making new banks, great or small, State or national. The same chains which those now existing to the center of this system of paper credit must equally fetter every similar institution we create. It is only by the extent to which this system has been pushed of late that we have been made fully aware of its irresistible tendency to subject our own banks and currency to a vast controlling power in a foreign land, and it adds a new argument to those which illustrate their precarious situation. Endangered in the first place by their own mismanagement and again by the conduct of every institution which connects them with the center of trade in our own country, they are yet subjected beyond all this to the effect of whatever measures policy, necessity, or caprice may induce those who control the credits of England to resort to. I mean not to comment upon these measures, present or past, and much less to discourage the prosecution of fair commercial dealings between the two countries, based on reciprocal benefits; but it having now been made manifest that the power of inflicting these and similar injuries is by the resistless law of a credit currency and credit trade equally capable of extending their consequences through all the ramifications of our banking system, and by that means indirectly obtaining, particularly when our banks are used as depositories of the public moneys, a dangerous political influence in the United States. I have deemed it my duty to bring the subject to your notice and ask for it your serious consideration. . . .

I am aware that the danger of inconvenience to the public and unreasonable pressure upon sound banks have been urged as objections to requiring the payment of the revenue in gold and silver. These objections have been greatly exaggerated. From the best estimates we may safely fix the amount of specie in the country at $85,000,000, and the portion of that which would be employed at any one time in the receipts and disbursements of the Government, even if the proposed change were made at once, would not, it is now, after fuller investigation, believed exceed four or five millions. If the change were gradual, several years would elapse before that sum would be required, with annual opportunities in the meantime to alter the law should experience prove it to be oppressive or inconvenient. The portions of the community on whose business the change would immediately operate are comparatively small, nor is it believed that its effect would be in the least unjust or injurious to them.

The ease and safety of the operations of the Treasury in keeping the public money are promoted by the application of its own drafts to the public dues. The objection arising from having them too long outstanding might be obviated and they yet made to afford to merchants and banks holding them an equivalent for specie, and in that way greatly lessen the amount actually required. Still less inconvenience will attend the requirement of specie in purchases of public lands. Such purchases, except when made on speculation, are in general but single transactions, rarely repeated by the same person; and it is a fact that for the last year and a half, during which the notes of sound banks have been received, more than a moiety of these payments has been voluntarily made in specie, being a larger proportion than would have been required in three years under the graduation proposed.

It is, moreover, a principle than which none is better settled by experience that the supply of the precious metals will always be found adequate to the uses for which they are required. They abound in countries where no other currency is allowed. In our own States, where small notes are excluded, gold and silver supply their place. When driven to their hiding places by bank suspensions, a little firmness in the community soon restores them in a sufficient quantity for ordinary purposes. Postage and other public dues have been collected in coin without serious inconvenience even in States where a depreciated paper currency has existed for years, and this, with the aid of Treasury notes for a part of the time, was done without interruption during the suspension of 1837. At the present moment the receipts and disbursements of the Government are made in legal currency in the largest portion of the Union. No one suggests a departure from this rule, and if it can now be successfully carried out it will be surely attended with even less difficulty when bank notes are again redeemed in specie.

Indeed, I can not think that a serious objection would anywhere be raised to the receipt and payment of gold and silver in all public transactions were it not from an apprehension that a surplus in the Treasury might withdraw a large portion of it from circulation and lock it up unprofitably in the public vaults. It would not, in my opinion, be difficult to prevent such an inconvenience from occurring; but the authentic statements which I have already submitted to you in regard to the actual amount in the public Treasury at any one time during the period embraced in them and the little probability of a different state of the Treasury for at least some years to come seem to render it unnecessary to dwell upon it. Congress, moreover, as I have before observed, will in every year have an opportunity to guard against it should the occurrence of any circumstances lead us to apprehend injury from this source. Viewing the subject in all its aspects, I can not believe that any period will be more auspicious than the present for the adoption of all measures necessary to maintain the sanctity of our own engagements and to aid in securing to the community that abundant supply of the precious metals which adds so much to their prosperity and gives such increased stability to all their dealings.

Fortunately for us at this moment, when the balance of trade is greatly against us and the difficulty of meeting it enhanced by the disturbed state of our money affairs, the bounties of Providence have come to relieve us from the consequences of past errors. A faithful application of the immense results of the labors of the last season will afford partial relief for the present, and perseverance in the same course will in due season accomplish the rest. We have had full experience in times past of the extraordinary results which can in this respect be brought about in a short period by the united and well-directed efforts of a community like ours. Our surplus profits, the energy and industry of our population, and the wonderful advantages which Providence has bestowed upon our country in its climate, its various productions, indispensable to other nations, will in due time afford abundant means to perfect the most useful of those objects for which the States have been plunging themselves of late in embarrassment and debt, without imposing on ourselves or our children such fearful burdens.

But let is be indelibly engraved on our minds that relief is not to be found in expedients. Indebtness can not be lessened by borrowing more money or by changing the form of the debt. The balance of trade is not to be turned in our favor by creating new demands upon us abroad. Our currency can not be improved by the creation of new banks or more issues from those which now exist. Although these devices sometimes appear to give temporary relief, they almost invariably aggravate the evil in the end. It is only by retrenchment and reform—by curtailing public and private expenditures, by paying our debts, and by reforming our banking system—that we are to expect effectual relief, security for the future, and an enduring prosperity. In shaping the institutions and policy of the General Government so as to promote as far as it can with its limited powers these important ends, you may rely on my most cordial cooperation.

M. VAN BUREN.

FOURTH ANNUAL MESSAGE
December 5, 1840

*After a review of the suspension of specie payments
at the outset of his term, "and the excesses in banking and commerce out of which it arose," and the
consequent losses to the government, Van Buren foc-
used on a theme which so characterized his administration; the importance of a pay-as-you-go financial
policy, avoiding indebtednesses. Among other things,
he saw foreign creditors as a threat to the "peace,
the honor, or the safety of the Republic." He answer-
ed as false charges of extravagance his foes made,
observing that in the few months the Independent
Treasury had functioned nothing had occurred to
challenge the successful anticipation of its friends.
Again he assailed the Whig proposal for a new Bank
on the ground that such financial power threatened
the political power of the people. To avoid a national
debt and maintain economy remained his theme. He
closed with an appeal to cut off trade with the nations who were maintaining "slave factories" on the
coast of Africa.*

WASHINGTON, December 5, 1840.

Fellow-Citizens of the Senate and House of Representatives:

Our devout gratitude is due to the Supreme Being for having graciously
continued to our beloved country through the vicissitudes of another year
the invaluable blessings of health, plenty, and peace. Seldom has this favored land been so generally exempted from the ravages of disease or the
labor of the husbandman more amply rewarded, and never before have
our relations with other countries been placed on a more favorable basis
than that which they so happily occupy at this critical conjuncture in the
affairs of the world. A rigid and persevering abstinence from all interference with the domestic and political relations of other States, alike due to
the genius and distinctive character of our Government and to the principles by which it is directed; a faithful observance in the management of
our foreign relations of the practice of speaking plainly, dealing justly,
and requiring truth and justice in return as the best conservatives of the
peace of nations; a strict impartiality in our manifestations of friendship
in the commercial privileges we concede and those we require from others
—these, accompanied by a disposition as prompt to maintain in every

emergency our own rights as we are from principle averse to the invasion of those of others, have given to our country and Government a standing in the great family of nations of which we have just cause to be proud and the advantages of which are experienced by our citizens throughout every portion of the earth to which their enterprising and adventurous spirit may carry them. Few, if any, remain insensible to the value of our friendship or ignorant of the terms on which it can be acquired and by which it can alone be preserved.

A series of questions of long standing, difficult in their adjustment and important in their consequences, in which the rights of our citizens and the honor of the country were deeply involved, have in the course of a few years (the most of them during the successful Administration of my immediate predecessor) been brought to a satisfactory conclusion; and the most important of those remaining are, I am happy to believe, in a fair way of being speedily and satisfactorily adjusted.

With all the powers of the world our relations are those of honorable peace. Since your adjournment nothing serious has occurred to interrupt or threaten this desirable harmony. If clouds have lowered above the other hemisphere, they have not cast their portentous shadows upon our happy shores. Bound by no entangling alliances, yet linked by a common nature and interest with the other nations of mankind, our aspirations are for the preservation of peace, in whose solid and civilizing triumphs all may participate with a generous emulation. Yet it behooves us to be prepared for any event and to be always ready to maintain those just and enlightened principles of national intercourse for which this Government has ever contended. In the shock of contending empires it is only by assuming a resolute bearing and clothing themselves with defensive armor that neutral nations can maintain their independent rights. . . .

The present sound condition of their finances and the success with which embarrassments in regard to them, at times apparently insurmountable, have been overcome are matters upon which the people and Government of the United States may well congratulate themselves. An overflowing Treasury, however it may be regarded as an evidence of public prosperity, is seldom conducive to the permanent welfare of any people, and experience has demonstrated its incompatibility with the salutary action of political institutions like those of the United States. Our safest reliance for financial efficiency and independence has, on the contrary, been found to consist in ample resources unencumbered with debt, and in this respect the Federal Government occupies a singularly fortunate and truly enviable position.

When I entered upon the discharge of my official duties in March, 1837, the act for the distribution of the surplus revenue was in a course of rapid execution. Nearly $28,000,000 of the public moneys were, in pursuance of its provisions, deposited with the States in the months of January, April, and July of that year. In May there occurred a general suspension of specie payments by the banks, including, with very few exceptions, those in which the public moneys were deposited and upon whose fidelity the Government had unfortunately made itself dependent for the revenues which had been collected from the people and were indispensable to the public service.

This suspension and the excesses in banking and commerce out of which it arose, and which were greatly aggravated by its occurrence, made to a great extent unavailable the principal part of the public money then on hand, suspended the collection of many millions accruing on merchants' bonds, and greatly reduced the revenue arising from customs and the public lands. These effects have continued to operate in various degrees to the present period, and in addition to the decrease in the revenue thus produced two and a half millions of duties have been relinquished by two biennial reductions under the act of 1833, and probably as much more upon the importation of iron for railroads by special legislation.

Whilst such has been our condition for the last four years in relation to revenue, we have during the same period been subjected to an unavoidable continuance of large extraordinary expenses necessarily growing out of past transactions, and which could not be immediately arrested without great prejudice to the public interest. Of these, the charge upon the Treasury in consequence of the Cherokee treaty alone, without adverting to others arising out of Indian treaties, has already exceeded $5,000,000; that for the prosecution of measures for the removal of the Seminole Indians, which were found in progress, has been nearly fourteen millions, and the public buildings have required the unusual sum of nearly three millions.

It affords me, however, great pleasure to be able to say that from the commencement of this period to the present day every demand upon the Government, at home or abroad, has been promptly met. This has been done not only without creating a permanent debt or a resort to additional taxation in any form, but in the midst of a steadily progressive reduction of existing burdens upon the people, leaving still a considerable balance of available funds which will remain in the Treasury at the end of the year. The small amount of Treasury notes, not exceeding $4,500,-000, still outstanding, and less by twenty-three millions than the United States have in deposit with the States, is composed of such only as are not yet due or have not been presented for payment. They may be redeemed out of the accruing revenue if the expenditures do not exceed the amount within which they may, it is thought, be kept without prejudice to the public interest, and the revenue shall prove to be as large as may justly be anticipated.

Among the reflections arising from the contemplation of these circumstances, one, not the least gratifying, is the consciousness that the Government had the resolution and the ability to adhere in every emergency to the sacred obligations of law, to execute all its contracts according to the requirements of the Constitution, and thus to present when most needed a rallying point by which the business of the whole country might be brought back to a safe and unvarying standard—a result vitally important as well to the interests as to the morals of the people. There can surely now be no difference of opinion in regard to the incalculable evils that would have arisen if the Government at that critical moment had suffered itself to be deterred from upholding the only true standard of value, either by the pressure of adverse circumstances or the violence of unmerited denunication. The manner in which the people sustained the performance of this duty was highly honorable to their fortitude and patriotism. It can not fail to stimulate their agents to adhere under all circumstances to the line of duty and to satisfy them of the safety with which a course really right and demanded by a financial crisis may in a community like ours be pursued, however apparently severe its immediate operation.

The policy of the Federal Government in extinguishing as rapidly as possible the national debt, and subsequently in resisting every temptation to create a new one, deserves to be regarded in the same favorable light. Among the many objections to a national debt, the certain tendency of public securities to concentrate ultimately in the coffers of foreign stockholders is one which is every day gathering strength. Already have the resources of many of the States and the future industry of their citizens been indefinitely mortgaged to the subjects of European Governments to the amount of twelve millions annually to pay the constantly accruing interest on borrowed money—a sum exceeding half the ordinary revenues of the whole United States. The pretext which this relation affords to foreigners to scrutinize the management of our domestic affairs, if not actually to intermeddle with them, presents a subject for earnest attention, not to say of serious alarm. Fortunately, the Federal Government, with the exception of an obligation entered into in behalf of the District of Columbia, which must soon be discharged, is wholly exempt from any such embarrassment. It is also, as is believed, the only Government which, having fully and faithfully paid all its creditors, has also relieved itself entirely from debt. To maintain a distinction so desirable and so honorable to our national character should be an object of earnest solicitude. Never should a free people, if it be possible to avoid it, expose themselves to the necessity of having to treat of the peace, the honor, or the safety of the Republic with the governments of foreign creditors, who, however well disposed they may be to cultivate with us in general friendly relations, are nevertheless by the law of their own condition made hostile to the success and permanency of political institutions like ours. Most humiliating may be the embarrassments consequent upon such a condition. Another objection, scarcely less formidable, to the commencement of a new debt is its inevitable tendency to increase in magnitude and to foster national extravagance.

He has been an unprofitable observer of events who needs at this day
to be admonished of the difficulties which a government habitually dependent on loans to sustain its ordinary expenditures has to encounter in
resisting the influences constantly exerted in favor of additional loans; by
capitalists, who enrich themselves by government securities for amounts
much exceeding the money they actually advance—a prolific source of
individual aggrandizement in all borrowing countries; by stockholders,
who seek their gains in the rise and fall of public stocks; and by the
selfish importunities of applicants for appropriations for works avowedly
for the accommodation of the public, but the real objects of which are
too frequently the advancement of private interests. The known necessity
which so many of the States will be under to impose taxes for the payment of the interest on their debts furnishes an additional and very cogent
reason why the Federal Government should refrain from creating a national debt, by which the people would be exposed to double taxation for
a similar object. We possess within ourselves ample resources for every
emergency, and we may be quite sure that our citizens in no future exigency will be unwilling to supply the Government with all the means asked
for the defense of the country. In time of peace there can, at all events,
be no justification for the creation of a permanent debt by the Federal
Government. Its limited range of constitutional duties may certainly under
such circumstances be performed without such a resort. It has, it is seen,
been avoided during four years of greater fiscal difficulties than have
existed in a similar period since the adoption of the Constitution, and
one also remarkable for the occurrence of extraordinary causes of expenditures.

But to accomplish so desirable an object two things are indispensable:
First, that the action of the Federal Government be kept within the boundaries prescribed by its founders, and, secondly, that all appropriations
for objects admitted to be constitutional, and the expenditure of them
also, be subjected to a standard of rigid but well-considered and practical
economy. The first depends chiefly on the people themselves—the opinions
they form of the true construction of the Constitution and the confidence
they repose in the political sentiments of those they select as their repre-
senatives in the Federal Legislature; the second rests upon the fidelity
with which their more immediate representatives and other public functionaries discharge the trusts committed to them. The duty of economizing
the expenses of the public service is admitted on all hands; yet there are
few subjects upon which there exists a wider difference of opinion than is
constantly manifested in regard to the fidelity with which that duty is
discharged. Neither diversity of sentiment nor even mutual recriminations
upon a point in respect to which the public mind is so justly sensitive
can well be entirely avoided, and least so at periods of great political
excitement. An intelligent people, however, seldom fail to arrive in the
end at correct conclusions in such a matter. Practical economy in the

management of public affairs can have no adverse influence to contend with more powerful than a large surplus revenue, and the unusually large appropriations for 1837 may without doubt, independently of the extraordinary requisitions for the public service growing out of the state of our Indian relations, be in no inconsiderable degree traced to this source. The sudden and rapid distribution of the large surplus then in the Treasury and the equally sudden and unprecedentedly severe revulsion in the commerce and business of the country, pointing with unerring certainty to a great and protracted reduction of the revenue, strengthened the propriety of the earliest practicable reduction of the public expenditures.

But to change a system operating upon so large a surface and applicable to such numerous and diversified interests and objects was more than the work of a day. The attention of every department of the Government was immediately and in good faith directed to that end, and has been so continued to the present moment. The estimates and appropriations for the year 1838 (the first over which I had any control) were somewhat diminished. The expenditures of 1839 were reduced $6,000,000. Those of 1840, exclusive of disbursements for public debt and trust claims, will probably not exceed twenty-two and a half millions, being between two and three millions less than those of the preceding year and nine or ten millions less than those of 1837. Nor has it been found necessary in order to produce this result to resort to the power conferred by Congress of postponing certain classes of the public works, except by deferring expenditures for a short period upon a limited portion of them, and which postponement terminated some time since—at the moment the Treasury Department by further receipts from the indebted banks became fully assured of its ability to meet them without prejudice to the public service in other respects. Causes are in operation which will, it is believed, justify a still further reduction without injury to any important national interest. The expenses of sustaining the troops employed in Florida have been gradually reduced through the persevering efforts of the War Department, and a reasonable hope may be entertained that the necessity for military operations in that quarter will soon cease. The removal of the Indians from within our settled borders is nearly completed. The pension list, one of the heaviest charges upon the Treasury, is rapidly diminishing by death. The most costly of our public buildings are either finished or nearly so, and we may, I think, safely promise ourselves a continued exemption from border difficulties.

The available balance in the Treasury on the 1st of January next is estimated at $1,500,000. This sum, with the expected receipts from all sources during the next year, will, it is believed, be sufficient to enable the Government to meet every engagement and have a suitable balance in the Treasury at the end of the year, if the remedial measures connected with the customs and the public lands heretofore recommended are adopted and the new appropriations by Congress shall not carry the expenditures beyond the official estimates.

The new system established by Congress for the safe-keeping of the public money, prescribing the kind of currency to be received for the public revenue and providing additional guards and securities against losses, has now been several months in operation. Although it might be premature upon an experience of such limited duration to form a definite opinion in regard to the extent of its influences in correcting many evils under which the Federal Government and the country have hitherto suffered, especially those that have grown out of banking expansions, a depreciated currency, and official defalcations, yet it is but right to say that nothing has occurred in the practical operation of the system to weaken in the slightest degree, but much to strengthen, the confident anticipations of its friends. The grounds of these have been heretofore so fully explained as to require no recapitulation. In respect to the facility and convenience it affords in conducting the public service, and the ability of the Government to discharge through its agency every duty attendant on the collection, transfer, and disbursement of the public money with promptitude and success, I can say with confidence that the apprehensions of those who felt it to be their duty to oppose its adoption have proved to be unfounded. On the contrary, this branch of the fiscal affairs of the Government has been, and it is believed may always be, thus carried on with every desirable facility and security. A few changes and improvements in the details of the system, without affecting any principles involved in it, will be submitted to you by the Secretary of the Treasury, and will, I am sure, receive at your hands that attention to which they may on examination be found to be entitled.

I have deemed this brief summary of our fiscal affairs necessary to the due performance of a duty specially enjoined upon me by the Constitution. It will serve also to illustrate more fully the principles by which I have been guided in reference to two contested points in our public policy which were earliest in their development and have been more important in their consequences than any that have arisen under our complicated and difficult, yet admirable, system of government. I allude to a national debt and a national bank. It was in these that the political contests by which the country has been agitated ever since the adoption of the Constitution in a great measure originated, and there is too much reason to apprehend that the conflicting interests and opposing principles thus marshaled will continue as heretofore to produce similar if not aggravated consequences.

Coming into office the declared enemy of both, I have earnestly endeavored to prevent a resort to either.

The consideration that a large public debt affords an apology, and produces in some degree a necessity also, for resorting to a system and extent of taxation which is not only oppressive throughout, but is likewise so apt to lead in the end to the commission of that most odious of all offenses against the principles of republican government, the prostitution of political power, conferred for the general benefit, to the aggrandizement of particular classes and the gratification of individual cupidity, is alone sufficient, independently of the weighty objections which have already been urged, to render its creation and existence the sources of bitter and unappeasable discord. If we add to this its inevitable tendency to produce and foster extravagant expenditures of the public moneys, by which a necessity is created for new loans and new burdens on the people, and, finally, refer to the examples of every government which has existed for proof, how seldom it is that the system, when once adopted and implanted in the policy of a country, has failed to expand itself until public credit was exhausted and the people were no longer able to endure its increasing weight, it seems impossible to resist the conclusion that no benefits resulting from its career, no extent of conquest, no accession of wealth to particular classes, nor any nor all its combined advantages, can counterbalance its ultimate but certain results—a splendid government and an impoverished people.

If a national bank was, as is undeniable, repudiated by the framers of the Constitution as incompatible with the rights of the States and the liberties of the people; if from the beginning it has been regarded by large portions of our citizens as coming in direct collision with that great and vital amendment of the Constitution which declares that all powers not conferred by that instrument on the General Government are reserved to the States and to the people; if it has been viewed by them as the first great step in the march of latitudinous construction, which unchecked would render that sacred instrument of as little value as an unwritten constitution, dependent, as it would alone be, for its meaning on the interested interpretation of a dominant party, and affording no security to the rights of the minority—if such is undeniably the case, what rational grounds could have been conceived for anticipating aught but determined opposition to such an institution at the present day.

Could a different result have been expected when the consequences which have flowed from its creation, and particularly from its struggles to perpetuate its existence, had confirmed in so striking a manner the apprehensions of its earliest opponents; when it had been so clearly demonstrated that a concentrated money power, wielding so vast a capital and combining such incalculable means of influence, may in those peculiar conjunctures to which this Government is unavoidably exposed prove an overmatch for the political power of the people themselves; when the true character of its capacity to regulate according to its will and its interests and the interests of its favorites the value and production of the labor and property of every man in this extended country had been so fully and fearfully developed; when it was notorious that all classes of this great community had, by means of the power and influence it thus possesses, been infected to madness with a spirit of heedless speculation;

when it had been seen that, secure in the support of the combination of influences by which it was surrounded, it could violate its charter and set the laws at defiance with impunity; and when, too, it had become most apparent that to believe that such an accumulation of powers can ever be granted without the certainty of being abused was to indulge in a fatal delusion?

To avoid the necessity of a permanent debt and its inevitable consequences I have advocated and endeavored to carry into effect the policy of confining the appropriations for the public service to such objects only as are clearly within the constitutional authority of the Federal Government; of excluding from its expenses those improvident and unauthorized grants of public money for works of internal improvement which were so wisely arrested by the constitutional interposition of my predecessor, and which, if they had not been so checked, would long before this time have involved the finances of the General Government in embarrassments far greater than those which are now experienced by any of the States; of limiting all our expenditures to that simple, unostentatious, and economical administration of public affairs which is alone consistent with the character of our institutions; of collecting annually from the customs, and the sales of public lands a revenue fully adequate to defray all the expenses thus incurred; but under no pretense whatsoever to impose taxes upon the people to a greater amount than was actually necessary to the public service conducted upon the principles I have stated.

I lieu of a national bank or a dependence upon banks of any description for the management of our fiscal affairs, I recommended the adoption of the system which is now in successful operation. That system affords every requisite facility for the transaction of the pecuniary concerns of the Government; will, it is confidently anticipated, produce in other respects many of the benefits whch have been from time to time expected from the creation of a national bank, but which never have been realized; avoid the manifold evils inseparable from such an institution; diminish to a greater extent that could be accomplished by any other measure of reform the patronage of the Federal Government—a wise policy in all governments, but more especially so in one like ours, which works well only in proportion as it is made to rely for its support upon the unbiased and unadulterated opinions of its constitutents; do away forever all dependence on corporate bodies either in the raising, collecting, safekeeping, or disbursing the public revenues, and place the Government equally above the temptation of fostering a dangerous and unconstitutional institution at home or the necessity of adapting its policy to the views and interests of a still more formidable money power abroad.

It is by adopting and carrying out these principles under circumstances the most arduous and discouraging that the attempt has been made, thus far successfully, to demonstrate to the people of the United States that a national bank at all times, and a national debt except it be incurred at a period when the honor and safety of the nation demand the temporary sacrifice of a policy which should only be abandoned in such exigencies, are not merely unnecessary, but in direct and deadly hostility to the principles of their Government and to their own permanent welfare.

The progress made in the development of these positions appears in the preceding sketch of the past history and present state of the financial concerns of the Federal Government. The facts there stated fully authorize the assertion that all the purposes for which this Government was instituted have been accomplished during four years of greater pecuniary embarrassment than were ever before experienced in time of peace, and in the face of opposition as formidable as any that was ever before arrayed against the policy of an Administration; that this has been done when the ordinary revenues of the Government were generally decreasing as well from the operation of the laws as the condition of the country, without the creation of a permanent public debt or incurring any liability other than such as the ordinary resources of the Government will speedily discharge, and without the agency of a national bank.

If this view of the proceedings of the Government for the period it embraces be warranted by the facts as they are known to exist; if the Army and Navy have been sustained to the full extent authorized by law, and which Congress deemed sufficient for the defense of the country and the protection of its rights and its honor; if its civil and diplomatic service has been equally sustained; if ample provision has been made for the administration of justice and the execution of the laws; if the claims upon public gratitude in behalf of the soldiers of the Revolution have been promptly met and faithfully discharged; if there have been no failures in defraying the very large expenditures growing out of that long-continued and salutary policy of peacefully removing the Indians to regions of comparative safety and prosperity; if the public faith has at all times and everywhere been most scrupulously maintained by a prompt discharge of the numerous, extended, and diversified claims on the Treasury—if all these great and permanent objects, with many others that might be stated, have for a series of years, marked by peculiar obstacles and difficulties, been successfully accomplished without a resort to a permanent debt or the aid of a national bank, have we not a right to expect that a policy the object of which has been to sustain the public service independently of either of these fruitful sources of discord will receive the final sanction of a people whose unbiased and fairly elicited judgment upon public affairs is never ultimately wrong?

That embarrassments in the pecuniary concerns of individuals of unexampled extent and duration have recently existed in this as in other commercial nations is undoubtedly true. To suppose it necessary now to trace these reverses to their sources would be a reflection on the intelligence of my fellow-citizens. Whatever may have been the obscurity in which the subject was involved during the earlier stages of the revulsion, there can not now be many by whom the whole question is not fully understood.

Not deeming it within the constitutional powers of the General Government to repair private losses sustained by reverses in business having no connection with the public service, either by direct appropriations from the Treasury or by special legislation designed to secure exclusive privileges and immunities to individuals or classes in preference to or at the expense of the great majority necessarily debarred from any participation in them, no attempt to do so has been either made, recommended, or encouraged by the present Executive.

It is believed, however, that the great purposes for the attainment of which the Federal Government was instituted have not been lost sight of. Intrusted only with certain limited powers, cautiously enumerated, distinctly specified, and defined with a precision arîd clearness which would seem to defy misconstruction, it has been my constant aim to confine myself within the limits so clearly marked out and so carefully guarded. Having always been of opinion that the best preservative of the union of the States is to be found in a total abstinence from the exercise of all doubtful powers on the part of the Federal Government rather than in attempts to assume them by a loose construction of the Constitution or an ingenious perversion of its words, I have endeavored to avoid recommending any measure which I had reason to apprehend would, in the opinion even of a considerable minority of my fellow-citizens, be regarded as trenching on the rights of the States or the provisions of the hallowed instrument of our Union. Viewing the aggregate powers of the Federal Government as a voluntary concession of the States, it seemed to me that such only should be exercised as were at the time intended to be given.

I have been strengthened, too, in the propriety of this course by the conviction that all efforts to go beyond this tend only to produce dissatisfaction and distrust, to excite jealousies, and to provoke resistance. Instead of adding strength to the Federal Government, even when successful they must ever prove a source of incurable weakness by alienating a portion of those whose adhesion is indispensable to the great aggregate of united strength and whose voluntary attachment is in my estimation far more essential to the efficiency of a government strong in the best of all possible strength—the confidence and attachment of all those who make up its constituent elements.

Thus believing, it has been my purpose to secure to the whole people and to every member of the Confederacy, by general, salutary, and equal laws alone, the benefit of those republican institutions which it was the end and aim of the Constitution to establish, and the impartial influence of which is in my judgment indispensable to their preservation. I can not bring myself to believe that the lasting happiness of the people, the prosperity of the States, or the permanency of their Union can be maintained by giving preference or priority to any class of citizens in the distribution of benefits or privileges, or by the adoption of measures which enrich one portion of the Union at the expense of another; nor can I see in the interference of the Federal Government with the local legislation and reserved rights of the States a remedy for present or a security against future dangers. . . .

The policy of the United States in regard to the Indians, of which a succinct account is given in my message of 1838, and of the wisdom and expediency of which I am fully satisfied, has been continued in active operation throughout the whole period of my Administration. Since the spring of 1837 more than 40,000 Indians have been removed to their new homes west of the Mississippi, and I am happy to add that all accounts concur in representing the result of this measure as eminently beneficial to that people.

The emigration of the Seminoles alone has been attended with serious difficulty and occasional bloodshed, hostilities having been commenced by the Indians in Florida until the apprehension that they would be compelled by force to comply with their treaty stipulations. The execution of the treaty of Paynes Landing, signed in 1832, but not ratified until 1834, was postponed at the solicitation of the Indians until 1836, when they again renewed their agreement to remove peaceably to their new homes in the West. In the face of this solemn and renewed compact they broke their faith and commenced hostilities by the massacre of Major Dade's command, the murder of their agent, General Thompson, and other acts of cruel treachery. . . .

Nothwithstanding the exertions of the experienced officers who had command there for eighteen months, on entering upon the administration of the Government I found the Territory of Florida a prey to Indian atrocities. A strenuous effort was immediately made to bring those hostilities to a close, and the army under General Jesup was reenforced until it amounted to 10,000 men, and furnished with abundant supplies of every description. In this campaign a great number of the enemy were captured and destroyed, but the character of the contest only was changed. The Indians, having been defeated in every engagement, dispersed in small bands throughout the country and became an enterprising, formidable, and ruthless banditti. General Taylor, who succeeded General Jesup, used his best exertions to subdue them, and was seconded in his efforts by the officers under his command; but he too failed to protect the Territory from their depredations. By an act of signal and cruel treachery they broke the truce made with them by General Macomb, who was sent from Washington for the purpose of carrying into effect the expressed wishes of Congress, and have continued their devastations ever since. General Armistead, who was in Florida when General Taylor left the army by permission, assumed the command, and after active summer operations was met by propositions for peace, and from the fortunate coincidence of the arrival in Florida at the same period of a delegation from the Seminoles who are happily settled west of the Mississippi and are now anxious to persuade their countrymen to join them there hopes were for some time entertained that the Indians might be induced to leave the Territory without further difficulty. These hopes have proved fallacious and hostilities have been renewed throughout the whole of the Territory. That this contest has endured so long is to be attributed to causes beyond the control of the Government. Experienced generals have had the command of the troops, officers and soldiers have alike distinguished themselves for their activity, patience, and enduring courage, the army has been constantly furnished with supplies of every description, and we must look for the causes which have so long procrastinated the issue of the contest in the vast extent of the theater of hostilities, the almost insurmountable obstacles presented by the nature of the country, the climate, and the wily character of the savages. . . .

The Navy, as will appear from the accompanying report of the Secretary, has been usefully and honorably employed in the protection of our commerce and citizens in the Mediterranean, the Pacific, on the coast of Brazil, and in the Gulf of Mexico. A small squadron, consisting of the frigate *Constellation* and the sloop of war *Boston*, under Commodore Kearney, is now on its way to the China and Indian seas for the purpose of attending to our interests in that quarter, and Commander Aulick, in the sloop of war *Yorktown*, has been instructed to visit the Sandwich and Society islands, the coasts of New Zealand and Japan, together with other ports and islands frequented by our whale ships, for the purpose of giving them countenance and protection should they be required. Other smaller vessels have been and still are employed in prosecuting the surveys of the coast of the United States directed by various acts of Congress, and those which have been completed will shortly be laid before you.

The exploring expedition at the latest date was preparing to leave the Bay of Islands, New Zealand, in further prosecution of objects which have thus far been successfully accomplished. The discovery of a new continent, which was first seen in latitude 66° 2' south, longitude 154° 27' east, and afterwards in latitude 66° 31' south, longitude 153°′40' east, by Lieutenants Wilkes and Hudson, for an extent of 1,800 miles, but on which they were prevented from landing by vast bodies of ice which encompassed it, is one of the honorable results of the enterprise. Lieutenant Wilkes bears testimony to the zeal and good conduct of his officers and men, and it is but justice to that officer to state that he appears to have performed the duties assigned him with an ardor, ability, and perseverance which give every assurance of an honorable issue to the undertaking. . . .

The suppression of the African slave trade has received the continued attention of the Government. The brig *Dolphin* and schooner *Grampus* have been employed during the last season on the coast of Africa for the purpose of preventing such portions of that trade as were said to be prosecuted under the American flag. After cruising off those parts of the coast most usually resorted to by slavers until the commencement of the rainy season, these vessels returned to the United States for supplies, and have since been dispatched on a similar service.

From the reports of the commanding officers it appears that the trade is now principally carried on under Portuguese colors, and they express the opinion that the apprehension of their presence on the slave coast has in a great degree arrested the prostitution of the American flag to this inhuman purpose. It is hoped that by continuing to maintain this force in that quarter and by the exertions of the officers in command much will be done to put a stop to whatever portion of this traffic may have been carried on under the American flag and to prevent its use in a trade which, while it violates the laws, is equally an outrage on the rights of others and the feelings of humanity. The efforts of the several Governments who are anxiously seeking to suppress this traffic must, however, be directed against the facilities afforded by what are now recognized as legitimate commercial pursuits before that object can be fully accomplished.

Supplies of provisions, water casks, merchandise, and articles connected with the prosecution of the slave trade are, it is understood, freely carried by vessels of different nations to the slave factories, and the effects of the factors are transported openly from one slave station to another without interruption or punishment by either of the nations to which they belong engaged in the commerce of that region. I submit to your judgments whether this Government, having been the first to prohibit by adequate penalties the slave trade, the first to declare it piracy, should not be the first also to forbid to its citizens all trade with the slave factories on the coast of Africa, giving an example to all nations in this respect which if fairly followed can not fail to produce the most effective results in breaking up those dens of iniquity.

M. VAN BUREN.

Bibliographical Aids

The emphasis in this and other volumes in the **Presidential Chronologies** series is on the administrations of the Presidents. Martin Van Buren's contributions as President, however, may be less important in historical retrospect than his role as a party builder and in the creation of Jacksonian Democracy. Therefore additional information has been added to the Chronology and titles included in the bibliography which reflect this part of Van Buren's life. Additional titles may be found in many of the books listed below, with Van Buren especially well treated by Robert V. Remini.

Asterisks after titles refer to books currently available in paperback editions.

SOURCE MATERIALS

The great bulk of Van Buren's papers are in the Library of Congress, undoubtedly having been carefully selected by Van Buren and heirs. They have not as yet appeared in book form, but are available on microfilm as part of the **Presidential Papers Microfilm** series. Some letters from Van Buren may be found in other collections, particularly in the New York Historical Society, the New York Public Library, and the New York State Library at Albany. Complete texts of Van Buren's messages to Congress may be found in Richardson as noted below.

Richardson, James D., ed. **Messages and Papers of the Presidents, 1789-1897.** Vol. III. Washington, D.C., 1896.

Van Buren, Martin. "The Autobiography of Martin Van Buren." Edited by John C. Fitzpatrick. Vol. II of the Annual **Report of the American Historical Association for the Year 1918.** Washington, D.C., 1920. A revealing portrait of the men and measures of the time as Van Buren saw them during his retirement. Unfortunately it only takes his career to 1834, during his Vice-Presidency.

————. **An Inquiry into Origin and Course of Political Parties in the United States.** New York, 1867. Also written late in his retirement and finished by his sons, this analysis is of particular interest in Van Buren's views of party loyalties and reasons therefore.

BIOGRAPHIES ON VAN BUREN

At this date there is no "definitive" biography of Van Buren which offers the student a thorough and judicious treatment of his life and presidency. Campaign biographies have been omitted for the obvious reason that they are especially biased.

Alexander, Holmes. **The American Talleyrand.** New York, 1935. A hostile, but readable work. Undocumented, and should be used with caution. Van Buren was also referred to as "The Little Magician" or "The Red Fox of Kinderhook" because of his political wiles.

Lynch, Denis T. **An Epoch and a Man: Martin Van Buren and His Times.** New York, 1929. The only other 20th century biographical work, and one of very limited usefulness. It is completely undocumented and uncritical.

Shepard, Edward M. **Martin Van Buren.** Boston, 1889. While the oldest volume cited, it remains the best although a sympathic treatment.

ESSAYS

Basset, John Spencer. "Martin Van Buren," in **American Secretaries of State,** edited by Samuel Flagg Bemis (New York, 1928), IV, 161-204.

Bretz, Julian P. "The Economic Background of the Liberty Party," **American Historical Review,** XXXIV (January, 1929), 250-264. Treats the rising problem of slavery in Van Buren's administration.

Carleton, W. G. "Political Aspects of the Van Buren Era," **South Atlantic Quarterly,** L (April, 1951), 167-185.

Duc Le, Thomas. "The Maine Frontier and the Northeastern Boundary Controversy," **American Historical Review,** LIII (October, 1947), 30-41.

Gatell, Frank O. "Sober Second Thoughts on Van Buren, The Albany Regency and the Wall Street Conspiracy," **Journal of American History,** LIII (June, 1966), 19-40.

Hale, Edward E. "Anecdotes of Martin Van Buren," **Outlook,** LXX (April 5, 1902), 849-852.

Meyers, Marvin. "Old Hero and Sly Fox: Variations on a Theme," in **The Jacksonian Persuasion.** Stanford, California, 1957.

Miley, Cora. "A Forgotten President, The Enigmatical 'Little Magician,' Martin Van Buren," **Americana,** XXIII (1929), 169-181.

Rayback, Joseph G. "Martin Van Buren's Break with James K. Polk," **New York History,** XXXIV (January, 1955), 51-62.

Remini, Robert V. "The Albany Regency," **New York History** (October, 1958), 341-355.

Rezneck, Samuel. "The Social History of an American Depression, 1837-1843," **American Historical Review,** XL (July, 1937), 662-687.

Shortridge, Wilson P. "The Canadian-American Frontier During the Rebellion of 1837-1838," **Canadian Historical Review**, VII (1926), 13-26.

Van Deusen, Glyndon G. "Some Aspects of Whig Thought and Theory in the Jacksonian Period," **American Historical Review**, LXIV (January, 1959), 305-322.

MONOGRAPHS AND SPECIAL AREAS

Benson, Lee. **The Concept of Jacksonian Democracy: New York as a Test Case.** Princeton, 1961.*

Dangerfield, George. **The Era of Good Feelings.** New York, 1952.* Pulitzer and Bancroft prize winner which interestingly shows the rise of party politics in which Van Buren played such an important role.

Donovan, Herbert D. A. **The Barnburners: A Study of the Internal Movements in the Political History of New York State, 1830-1852.** New York, 1952.

Hammond, Bray. **Banks and Politics in America from the Revolution to the Civil War.** Princeton, 1957.*

Hofstadter, Richard. **The American Political Tradition and the Men Who Made It.** New York, 1948.*

Kinley, David. **The Independent Treasury of the United States and Its Relations to the Banks of the Country.** Washington, 1910.

McCormick, Richard P. **The Second American Party System: Party Formation in the Jacksonian Era.** Chapel Hill, South Carolina, 1966.*

McGrave, Charles. **The Panic of 1837.** Chicago, 1924.

Meyers, Marvin. **The Jacksonian Persuasion: Politics and Belief.** Stanford, California, 1957.*

Nance, J. M. **After Jacente.** New York, 1963. A recent treatment of Texas from 1836-1842, another important topic in Van Buren's public life.

Remini, Robert V. **Andrew Jackson and the Bank War.** New York, 1967.*

Schlesinger, Arthur M., Jr. **The Age of Jackson.** Boston, 1946.* A Pulitzer prize study which contains many significant items about Van Buren both in relation to Jackson and during his own administration. It also treats Van Buren (and his son John) during the final years of Jacksonianism in the 1840's and 1850's.

Tocqueville, Alexis de. **Democracy in America.** New York, 1954.* This perceptive Frenchman gives the reader a deep insight into Jacksonian America that is almost unique.

Turner, Frederick Jackson. **The United States, 1830-1850.** New York, 1935.* A study of sectional influences at work upon the political history of the period.

Van Deusen, Glyndon G. **The Jacksonian Era: 1828-1848.** New York, 1959.* Not a new interpretation of the era, but a synthesis of the divergent insights of other historians. This is an expertly executed brief summary of the best scholarship; a standard one-volume treatment of the subject.

White, Leonard D. **The Jacksonians: A Study in Administrative History, 1829-1861.** New York, 1954.* Excellent on Jackson, but fails to do justice to Van Buren's role.

RELATED BIOGRAPHIES

Bemis, Samuel F. **John Quincy Adams and the Union.** New York, 1956.

Bobbe, Dorothie. **De Witt Clinton.** New York, 1933.

Chambers, William N. **Old Bullion Benton, Senator from the New West.** Boston, 1956.

Coit, Margaret L. **John C. Calhoun.** Boston, 1950.*

Current, Richard N. **Daniel Webster and the Rise of National Conservatism.** Boston, 1955.*

Eaton, Clement. **Henry Clay and the Art of American Politics.** Boston, 1957.

Garraty, John Arthur. **Silas Wright.** New York, 1949.

Govan, Thomas. **Nicholas Biddle.** Chicago, 1959.

Remini, Robert V. **Andrew Jackson.** New York, 1966.*

Sellers, Charles G. **James K. Polk, Jacksonian.** Princeton, 1957.

Spencer, I. D. **The Victor and the Spoils: A Life of William L. Marcy.** New York, 1959.

Van Deusen, Glydon G. **The Life of Henry Clay.** Boston, 1939.

————. **Thurlon Weed, Wizard of the Lobby.** Boston, 1947.

————. **William Henry Seward.** New York, 1967.

Wiltse, Charles M. **John C. Calhoun.** 3 vols. Indianapolis, 1944-1951.

Woodford, John B. **Lewis Cass, the Last Jeffersonian.** New Brunswick, 1950.

THE PRESIDENCY

Bailey, Thomas A. **Presidential Greatness: The Image and the Man from George Washington to the Present.** New York, 1966.* Rates Van Buren as a better President than popularly believed.

Binkley, Wilfred E. **The Man in the White House: His Powers and Duties.** Revised ed. New York, 1964.* Treats the development of the various roles of the president.

Brown, Stuart Gerry. **The American Presidency: Leadership, Partisanship, and Popularity.** New York, 1966.*

Burns, James MacGregor. **Presidential Government: The Crucible of Leadership.** New York, 1966.*

Corwin, Edward S. **The President: Office and Powers.** 4th revised ed. New York, 1957.* An older classic.

Cunliffe, Marcus. **The American Heritage History of the Presidency.** New York, 1968. A recent interpretation by a competent authority. Contains excerpts from Representative Charles Ogle's speech in 1840 attacking Van Buren's supposed royal habits.

Haight, David E. & Johnston, Larry D. **The President: Roles and Powers.** Chicago, 1965.* Essays on the presidency by both presidents and other experts.

Israel, Fred L., ed. **The State of the Union Messages of the Presidents. 1790-1966.** New York, 1967. Contains introduction by Arthur M. Schlesinger, Jr.

Kane, Joseph Nathan. **Facts about the Presidents.** Revised ed. New York, 1968.* Useful, with complete information on the President's family, nominating conventions, and cabinet appointments. Includes comparative as well as biographical data about the presidents.

Koenig, Louis W. **The Chief Executive.** New York, 1964. Authoritative study of presidential powers.

Laski, Harold J. **The American Presidency.** New York, 1940.* A classic.

Roseboom, Eugene H. **A History of Presidential Elections.** Revised ed. New York, 1964.

Rossiter, Clinton. **The American Presidency.** 2nd ed. New York, 1960.* A standard treatment by an outstanding authority.

NAME INDEX

116

TITLES IN THE OCEANA
PRESIDENTIAL CHRONOLOGY SERIES

Reference books containing Chronology — Documents — Bibliographical
Aids for each President covered.
Series Editor: Howard F. Bremer

1. GEORGE WASHINGTON   96 pages/$3.00
   edited by Howard F. Bremer

2. JOHN ADAMS   96 pages/$3.00
   edited by Howard F. Bremer

3. JAMES BUCHANAN   96 pages/$3.00
   edited by Irving J. Sloan

4. GROVER CLEVELAND   128 pages/$4.00
   edited by Robert I. Vexler

5. FRANKLIN PIERCE   96 pages/$3.00
   edited by Irving J. Sloan

6. ULYSSES S. GRANT   128 pages/$4.00
   edited by Philip R. Moran

7. MARTIN VAN BUREN   128 pages/$4.00
   edited by Irving J. Sloan

8. THEODORE ROOSEVELT   128 pages/$4.00
   edited by Gilbert Black

9. BENJAMIN HARRISON*   96 pages/$3.00
   edited by Harry J. Sievers

10. JAMES MONROE   96 pages/$3.00
    edited by Ian Elliot

11. WOODROW WILSON*   128 pages/$4.00
    edited by Robert Vexler

12. RUTHERFORD B. HAYES   96 pages/$3.00
    edited by Arthur Bishop

13. ANDREW JACKSON*   128 pages/$4.00
    edited by Ronald Shaw

14. WARREN HARDING*   96 pages/$3.00
    edited by Philip Moran

*Available June, 1969

Books may be ordered from
OCEANA PUBLICATIONS, INC.
Dobbs Ferry, New York 10522